Sins of Pearl

By

Jim Henry

This book is a work of fiction. Places, events, and situations in this story are purely fictional. Any resemblance to actual persons, living or dead, is coincidental.

ISBN: 1-4107-3390-4 (e-book)
ISBN: 1-4107-3389-0 (Paperback)
ISBN: 1-4107-7070-2 (Dust Jacket)

Library of Congress Control Number: 2003092643

This book is printed on acid free paper.

Printed in the United States of America
Bloomington, IN

1stBooks - rev. 6/23/03

PEARL

A smooth, rounded, variously tinted nacreous concretion formed as a deposit around a foreign body in the shells of various sea mollusks, and largely used as a gem. Most come in various shades of white, but pearls of color are just as valuable, and sometimes more.

Most of today's pearls are cultured in farms in the world's azure oceans. Simply put, pearl farmers implant plain seeds in oysters, which, over time and with careful nurturing, manufacture skins of varying colors, each ultimately giving birth to gem-quality pearl.

ACKNOWLEDGMENTS

I would like to thank **George Corbe** and **Skip Gregory** of Florida's Agency for Health Care Administration Office of Plans and Construction for initiating my first visit to Haiti, and to **Larry Smith**, electrical engineer, and **Matt Harrell**, architect, for being part of the original team, and to **Jim Ketchen**, who spent his vacation installing a medical air system at the University Hospital in Port-au-Prince.

.

Cover
created by

Sherry Pentecost, a Georgia Bulldog peach.

DEDICATIONS

This novel is dedicated to Franck St. Come; Kesnel Vertil; Marlene Charlotin; members of the Rotary Clubs of Sarasota, Florida, USA, and Port-au-Prince, Haiti; employees and agents of the United States Agency for International Development; and to all the citizens of Haiti who are working to make our world a better place to live.

Because of the commitment of the above individuals and organizations, a minimum of 25 percent of the profits generated by this novel will be set aside in a Caribbean Basin Fund to support humanitarian, educational, and cultural projects in the Basin, and in Latin and South America, with priority given to initiatives in Haiti and the Dominican Republic. The Caribbean Initiative will be managed by the Sarasota Rotary Foundation, and distributed through programs of the Rotary Foundation, a nonprofit corporation that supports the efforts of Rotary International to achieve world peace through humanitarian, educational, and cultural programs.

Jim Henry

Dance to the rhythm of the universe,
and you dance with eternal spirits.
Dance to the rhythm of time and space,
and you dance alone.

Jim Henry, 2001

Jim Henry

Point St. Marc, Haiti

Pearl Maura Johnson

"Mother! I just don't understand why a bright person like you can't let go! He's an ass! Simple as that!" Beverly glared at her mother. "And people who lord that type of control over others aren't any better! You have to break yourself loose to really be free and equal!" She whirled and stormed out the door. "You are responsible only for yourself."

Before the door slammed, Pearl's eyes snapped open. She bolted upright. Her heart pounded. *The same nightmare.* Then the caldron inside her overflowed and, like molten lava, heat spread throughout her body. The leaden blanket of malaise engulfed her. Her heart shook as blood rushed to her skin in a futile attempt to ward off the inevitable hot flash. Perspiration popped from every pore. Her thighs stuck together.

She moved aside the linen cover, parted the mosquito netting, and forced her naked legs over the edge of the bed. The terrazzo floor cooled her feet. *Maybe she should lie on it for a while?* No. Slippery when wet.

The oppressive air worsened her meltdown. She glanced hopefully at the idle paddle fan suspended from the twelve-foot ceiling. No movement. No stored electricity. Longing for some refreshing cross-ventilation, her eyes scanned lace curtains dressing the high windows. Nothing. The display on the battery-powered clock radio read 4:53.

She sighed and hefted herself from the bed, struggled to the old mahogany table that doubled as a desk, lifted the white insulated pitcher, poured a bit of precious ice water on a washcloth, placed it gently over her face, and drew deep, controlled breaths. Cool, moist air rushed into her overflowing kettle. Droplets of refreshing liquid trickled down her skin. She repeated the process, then dabbed her body with the damp cloth.

Pearl stood in front of the insect-screen-covered rear window of the room hoping to catch a waft of air. Nothing. She unfolded an oversized oriental fan and, with long, sweeping strokes, created her own breeze, and wondered if the energy expended fanning herself created more perspiration than it evaporated. She didn't really care. Any momentary relief was welcome.

Five hours of uninterrupted sleep. Thank God for little things. The next power surge should be when school was in session. Finally, as she knew it would, her own personal heat wave slowly evaporated. She prayed that Wayne hadn't forgotten the estrogen.

She lifted the insect screen and stuck her head out the window. Bright stars flickered in the northwestern sky. She scanned the heavens from west to east. The stars' lights dimmed as the sky faded from black to purple, blended into sapphire blue, and ultimately gave way to the aqua and orange ripples emanating from the saffron aura silhouetting Mt. Bonhomme. When she arrived in Haiti three years earlier, she had difficulty adjusting to how early daylight came. By six the day would be bright. And hot.

To extinguish the remaining embers, Pearl dampened the cloth once more and swathed her breasts while standing before a wall-hung, three-quarter length muddle-edged mirror that reflected its age more than hers. She wondered why men thought women's breasts were sensuous. Ted, her estranged husband, used to rub them as a prelude to sex. She couldn't remember why. She got absolutely nothing out of it, but he must have. Since it was her duty to submit to her husband, she had allowed it. On their honeymoon, while suffering from morning sickness, she tried to talk with him about sex and her lack of enjoyment. He huffed and barked that it was her problem, not his. End of conversation. End of togetherness. For the next thirty-one years they shared space, money, a little sex, and two children.

As the sun peeked over the mountain, the school's rooster confirmed the eternal circular nature of time. A sunbeam streamed through the window and bathed her face. She examined her features. The toll of bygone years, including the scar on her temple, was no longer cloaked in darkness. Many people, including Ted, had told her she was pretty. She didn't believe it. He, and others, used to say that, except for her rusty hair, she resembled Cheryl Ladd, the actress in the old television program *Charlie's Angels*. Pearl smiled. She didn't think Cheryl Ladd would ever have crow's feet or a sagging chin. A mosquito buzzed by her ear and landed on her bare shoulder. She slapped it into eternity. "Sorry," she mumbled. Mosquitoes were constant companions.

Pearl grabbed a towel and dried from her body what sweat had not evaporated. As she slipped into her white cotton underwear, the school's generator woke up. Still, no government power. The paddle fan lurched, stopped, then lumbered into a slow, constant rotation. Today she would turn it off. She had left it on yesterday, which was why the inverter serving her room had not fully charged. The fan had stopped just after midnight.

She opened the cedar-lined oak wardrobe, which had seen many more years than she, thumbed through the twelve hangers, and selected a bright yellow sun dress that blossomed with deep red hibiscus blooms. The waist resisted passing over her shoulders, but, with a gentle hitch, it settled comfortably into place. Standing before the mirror, she adjusted the side of the waistband, then turned completely around checking the hem. Satisfied that it was straight, she studied her profile.

A fly buzzed by her and landed on the mirror.

She brushed her hands over the top of her derriere, smoothing the fluffs. The fly seemed purposely to follow her hand's reflection. "Must be male," she mumbled. The dress was a bit snug but otherwise almost a perfect fit. At least it didn't tuck under her bigger-than-she-wanted butt. Before and just after they married, Ted liked to pat it. That, she didn't mind. The obligation that usually followed was what she grew to dread. Thank goodness he finally lost interest.

The fly took wing.

Natural daylight slowly bathed the room. She had to lower the slat shutters on the two windows facing the sun before the room became unbearable. As she leaned over the table to close the second set of shutters, she stubbed her toe. Water sloshed from a tumbler she had left from grading papers the night before. "Damn!" She quickly grabbed the towel and wiped up the spill before it could work its way into a stack of papers. Then she examined and flexed her toes. No permanent damage.

A white wicker chest beside her twin bed doubled as a night stand. She kept most of her underwear and a few cosmetics and personal necessities in three small top drawers. The two larger drawers held most of her casual outer garments. When weather dictated that she stay indoors, her sanctuary—a cushioned, wooden rocking chair and floor lamp with a yellowing shade— sat in the corner between the dresser and wardrobe. A ginger-colored circular woven straw rug in the middle of the floor completed the room's furnishings. The only decoration on the creamy-hued concrete block walls was an ivory-on-ebony crucifix hanging over the bed.

Her clock radio sat on the wicker chest facing the bed. A rectangular white lace doily, a gift from Michelette, a prized student, covered the middle, and a small battery-powered music box that, when opened, chimed "Morning Has Broken" occupied the other end. On the doily sat three small portraits in matching natural wood frames. The one near the radio was of Rose (the thirty-five-year-old sister whom Pearl practically raised, their mother having died when the child was only four). In the middle was Beverly, her thirty-year-old daughter, and on the right, Wayne, her thirty-three-year-old son, whom she was meeting the next evening at la Villa Creole in Pétionville, a suburb of Port-au-Prince. Both were unmarried—a legacy, Pearl reasoned, of her own marriage.

Whomp, whomp, whomp, sounded the thuds of the log drum announcing breakfast. Pearl quickly rolled up the mosquito netting, made her bed, ran a brush through her hair, and checked that the scar, a legacy of her last disagreement with Ted, was hidden. It wasn't. She dabbed on a touch of base, rubbed it in, dusted it with powder, and reexamined it. No one had noticed the scar, or at least no one had asked about it. Satisfied with her cover-up, she slipped on her shoes and, anxious to see the students, stepped briskly onto the campus of St. Jude's Catholic School. The past three years had been the happiest of her adult life.

The campus, at the base of St. Jude's Peninsula, was nestled between Mud Crab Bay on the east and the Gulf of Gonave on the west. An eight-foot-high tan concrete wall surrounded its five concrete block, ivory buildings. The Nest, the building that housed the female staff, was near the rear wall. According to legend, the name was shortened from "Old Crow's Nest."

A white-robed nun, picking hybrid, pumpkin-colored daffodils from the Nest's flower garden, joined Pearl on the crushed shell path. "Good morning, Pearl," she said, speaking as fast as the wings on the humming bird that zipped by. "Isn't it a glorious day?"

"Bonjour, Sister Joan. It certainly is."

Sister Joan, from France, was about Pearl's height and always had a genuine smile. She never told her age, but Pearl guessed her to be about forty. The nun had been teaching at St. Jude's eleven years. She classified herself as thin, but Moland, the school's antithesis of a typical janitor, said that if she turned sideways she could hide behind a sugarcane stalk. Like fields of cane, she was always in motion, full of nervous energy. Pearl envied Sister Joan. She never gained an ounce, yet she put away twice as much food.

The two walked briskly past the Classrooms, a functionally identified building, located on the bay side of the campus. The path took them between the Louvre, the student toilet facilities adjacent to the Classrooms, and the aptly named Kitchen. A breeze-way, raised six steps to the Kitchen's floor level, separated it from Primal Hall, affectionately called because it was the first building at the school and served one of the staff's primordial needs—eating.

Pearl held the door to the dining room, the largest space in Primal Hall, for Sister Joan. Natti, the school's cook and general housekeeper, had already stocked the rotating center of the round mahogany table with fresh orange juice, milk, water, coffee, a plate of fresh mango slices, a basket of homemade raisin muffins, and a cup of sugar. The table comfortably sat ten, so it was downright roomy when seating only the staff, which included Father Mike, the parish priest, principal-in-charge, and main disciplinarian; Sister Marie, the schoolmistress, who actually ran the school as well as taught the first three levels; Sister Joan, a secondary teacher and friend to everyone; Sister Ester, who taught the fourth through sixth level and acted as school counselor; Pearl, who also taught secondary level as well as English and anything else deemed necessary; and Moland, the caretaker, janitor, vocational instructor, and jack-of-all-trades. Natti, welcome to sit at the table, usually found it more convenient to eat at a different time.

"Good morning," Father Mike said as Sister Joan placed the daffodils in a vase on a small table. The blossoms pointed to a wooden crucifix hanging on the wall.

"Good morning," the staff replied.

"Moland," Father Mike said, "I believe it's your turn."

The lean, baldheaded, wizened sixty or seventy something with a pocked, Brazil nut complexion nodded. All heads bowed. "Thanks, Almighty," his bass voice articulated, "for allowing us to participate in this cycle of life, for the living entities that have died so that we may live, and for my being allowed to share moments in eternity with all those around this table. And all said . . . "

"Amen."

"Who would like eggs for breakfast?" Natti asked, not waiting for the echoes to die. A pure African, Natti was barely five feet tall, slender, and had short, silvery hair, bright eyes, and a sharp wit. No one, even she, knew her exact age, but everyone guessed somewhere in the seventies. She lived in a small room off the kitchen, and, best as anyone could decipher, had had five children, all deceased. Natti never talked about her man, or men. She always said she thanked the Lord for giving her the family she now had and loved—the school's staff and children.

"Two eggs over," replied Father Mike. "Toast. No bacon."

Natti nodded and looked at Sister Joan, who, munching a muffin, ordered her standard feast, "Two eggs, sunny-side up, three slices of bacon, and two pieces of wheat toast."

"Sunny-side up not good in Haiti," Natti replied. "Eggs will be cooked." She looked at Sisters Marie and Ester, who both asked for their usual. Natti acknowledged and looked at Moland. "Three slices of toast, peanut butter, and a banana."

"Miss Pearl?" Natti asked.

"Do we have bananas?"

"Yes, ma'am," Natti answered. "Fried?"

Pearl loved Natti's fried bananas but recalled her reflection. She hesitated, then decided to worry about the hips and thighs later. "Yes, please! And two slices of wheat toast."

Natti smiled. She knew why the hesitation. As she shuffled out to the kitchen, she whispered loud enough for all to hear, "I go light on the coconut oil!"

They ate well, thanks to the large garden and chickens that Moland kept behind the classrooms, where he also taught agriculture and poultry farming. He had the students clean the chicken pen each day and kept a compost heap just outside the leeward wall. He and Natti traded eggs and chickens for pork and other staples.

"Well," Sister Marie said, "is there anything going on today that I should know?" Like Sister Joan, Sister Marie hailed from France. She had just turned fifty and was fluent in English, French, and Creole. Brutally efficient, her steely eyes and tight features masked a gentle heart and unparalleled compassion.

"Just a reminder," Pearl said. "Moland is driving me into Port-au-Prince tomorrow afternoon and picking me up Monday. I'm stopping by the printer's to get a proof of our book, so if there's anything I can do for anyone, please say so." She had written down several local oral legends and, with Sister Marie's and Moland's help, translated them into Creole.

"How about getting us a five hundred or better Pentium computer?" Sister Ester asked. "The DX two-sixty-six, even though it's speeded up, is horrendously slow." Everyone chuckled. Computers and uninterruptible power supplies were on everyone's list. Only Sister Ester and Father Mike had them, and until they got more money, none could be purchased.

"Since you're going to the bookstore," Sister Joan said, "my kids could use some more pencils." St. Jude's students had sponsors in the United States and Europe, but supplies still ran thin.

"If we have the money," piped up Sister Marie, "we need some composition books." She looked at Father Mike.

"I believe we can get a few," he said. "Put them on our account."

"Good," Sister Marie replied. "Get twenty."

Pearl looked around. "Anything else?" Everyone shook their heads.

"What's on for the secondary students today?" Sister Marie asked, looking at Sister Joan and Pearl.

"Francois's coming in to evaluate art the students have completed during the past three weeks," Pearl answered. Everyone knew "evaluate" wasn't exactly what Francois did. She instructed, guided, cajoled, praised, and critiqued all of the arts and crafts the students prepared, regardless of difficulty. She expected them to look beyond their being, into the transcendent. Francois was good. The students, Pearl, Father Mike, Sister Joan, Natti, and Moland looked forward to her coming. Sisters Marie and Ester were tolerant, bowing to her local popularity, national fame, and the fact that she was one of the school's major benefactors.

Sister Marie looked at Moland.

"Sometime today or tomorrow I'm going into St. Marc to arrange diesel for the generator," he said. "And unless we get some rain, our main water tank will be empty by Saturday, and, by Sunday, so will the one in town." He looked at Father Mike. "I think I better get them filled." These tanks were the only freshwater supplies for the 4,000 plus citizens of the surrounding area.

"How much?" Father Mike asked.

"About a hundred ninety dollars, I suspect," Moland replied. "No rain for over two weeks. And the Nest cistern is almost empty. Without rain today, you ladies will have to bathe at the beach or take spit baths." He looked at Father Mike. "Got less than three day's in the Primal cistern."

Father Mike cracked a smile. "And the folks back home in Cleveland think that because we live in the tropics we get lots of rain. They don't understand that most of Haiti is semiarid."

"The same with my family!" Pearl said.

Natti entered bearing a loaded serving tray that looked as big around as she was tall.

The Artists

After breakfast, Pearl left Primal Hall and walked over to the Shelter, a large open-air structure situated on the campus's east side just inside Francois's Wall, the portion of the front security wall that separated the campus from the parking lot. The wall got its name because it was where Francois, the now famous artist but former cantankerous student, frequently used graffiti to express her many and usually controversial opinions. It was also where, according to local lore, a critic and gallery owner chanced by and observed the fourteen-year-old, brushes in hand and several open containers of paint on the ground, angrily depicting her thoughts regarding a recent punitive dismissal from class. The critic recognized immediately that the intensity and perception of Francois's work spoke to all ages and epitomized the Haitian belief that art transcends life and turns suffering into harmony.

When confident she wouldn't get a brush filled with paint swiped across her face, the critic interrupted the girl's expressionism, managed to get a look at some of her abstracts, and offered to show them in Pétionville. Francois, it is said, never again entered the campus as a student. Francois's Wall was now where the students and, with the school's permission, other aspiring artists exhibited various works for public sale.

The Shelter, with its fifteen-foot-high ceiling and three open sides, was an ideal multipurpose facility. Its high peak served as home for a small colony of bats. Pearl had not observed the nesting mammals until Moland pointed them out while teaching the staff and students natural forms of insect control.

On special days, when the chapel in Primal Hall was too small, worship services convened in the Shelter. Today, it would serve as an art gallery. Pearl expected Michelette Alouidor, whom Francois considered a prodigy, to be the first student in, but chestnut-skinned Jean Claude LaPorte, a likable, eleventh level student from St. Marc, stood beside an automobile differential and axle housing that was, except for the bolts, striped with psychedelic colors. The bolts were painted unfamiliar shades. The piece reminded Pearl of the sixties' flower children. She withheld a chuckle, knowing that Francois would find something meaningful in it.

Both Pearl and Jean Claude recognized the soft voice calling for help and went to assist. Michelette stood at the front gate waiting for someone to open it. A rainbow-striped blue backpack with an empty five-gallon plastic water bottle hanging from it drooped from her shoulders, and she held a framed canvas almost as big as her outstretched arms.

Jean Claude, several inches taller than Michelette, took hold of the thirteen-year-old's drawing. "Let me carry it."

"Thanks, but be careful. It's charcoal. It will smear cause I didn't have any spray."

Pearl untied the water bottle as the gate swung closed. "Bugs got into our good water and the cistern's dry," Michelette said. "I have to take some home."

Michelette was tall for her age, and her smooth, bronze athletic body showed the signs of maturing. Long, black eyelashes complemented her sparkling, brown eyes. A dimple punctuated each cheek. Today she wore her silky, waist-length, jet-black hair in braids.

"Where do you want me to set this?" Jean Claude asked.

Michelette looked around, studied the sun and shadows, then chose a place near one of the two center columns where the natural light would be even throughout the day. She brushed away a deserted spider web. "Right here." She placed one hand on the floor and patted the column with the other. Jean Claude knew she meant that exact spot and carefully followed her instructions. She made minor adjustments in the way he propped the drawing. When satisfied, she walked over to his differential housing and examined it carefully. "Smooth flow of energy in the paint, maybe showing the type work this thing does."

A dazzling white smile flashed across Jean Claude's face.

While Michelette and Jean Claude chatted, Pearl studied the charcoal, a typical Haitian plantation scene surrounded by abstract impressions. In the foreground, workers on ladders harvested mangos while field hands toiled in the distance collecting bananas. At the top

left, small fat black caricatures of the plantation's
owners looked down on the workers. Along the sides
and at the bottom Michelette depicted women, lots of
women, all with babies strapped to them as they toiled
at various stages of housekeeping, tending gardens,
cutting wood, and making and selling charcoal. The
last figure, in the right upper corner, portrayed a
lumpy, emaciated woman, surrounded by chunks of
charcoal, ascending into heaven, leaving behind three
small children with outstretched arms. Pearl sniffed
and flicked a tear from her cheek.

Michelette walked up. "Do you like it?"

Pearl knew that it made no difference whether she
liked it or not. Michelette always expressed what she
felt. "It's moving, Michelette, really moving. When did
you do it?"

"Last Saturday and Sunday when I was watching
Mama make briquettes. It just came out of me. I hope
Francois likes it." Michelette's mother, Laura, like
many Haitian women, eked out a living as a housemaid
in two beach houses on the southern coast of Point St.
Marc, near the old Club Med. She supplemented their
income by making and selling charcoal, a task fraught
with exposure to carcinogens. Two of Laura's friends,
both with small children, had recently died from
cancer.

Another student, fifteen-year-old Girard Louis,
came in with a rifle carved from the stringy trunk of a
coconut palm and a beautifully painted shrunken
human head crafted from coconut husks. He was a
bright, troubled boy who took to the computer like a
bat homing in on a mosquito, and had devoured the

relics on campus before they had been there two days. Without a challenge, the staff feared they would not be able to keep him focused and that he would be another in Haiti's long list of wasted brainpower. Sullen, he set his work down and joined Jean Claude and Michelette.

Six more students brought in work that varied from simple painted shells to a complicated stick building. Pearl met each student and studied their piece, being careful not to single one out. Each was special. The students looked over each other's work, made encouraging remarks, then, as if drawn by a magnet, congregated around Michelette and chitchatted like the teenagers they were. All except Girard. He stood outside the group's perimeter and listened.

The chattering halted at the familiar staccato of Francois's Suzuki Samurai, which stopped just outside the wall. Her sculpted, lithe five-foot-four body illustrated confidence in motion as bare feet transported her through the iron gate. She wore splotched, rolled-up Levis and a paint-streaked, three-quarter sleeve, denim shirt tied just beneath her firm, braless breasts. Dark brown Cleopatra-style hair framed her smooth, soft, milk chocolate complexion. An impish smile and bright onyx eyes portrayed her personality.

"How is everybody?" she asked.

The students answered in unison, then, knowing the routine, fanned out and stood beside their work. Francois looked around and counted, then looked at Pearl, smiled, and, as always, asked, "Where's yours?"

"When I become as talented as these students," she replied, "I'll do something." She tried to have a different answer every time.

"Talent is secondary." Francois tapped herself on the chest. "It's what one lets out from in here that counts." Her attention shifted immediately to Girard's rifle. She picked it up, examined the cuts, looked at the proportions, then lifted the shrunken head and studied it. She looked at Girard. "Oh, I see many things here." Her smile waned. "Most important, in this head, I see helplessness and lack of desire. Then, in the weapon, the craving for power. Want to talk about it?"

A smile almost cracked Girard's oak-colored, solemn face. He shook his head. Francois had nailed him right on. He was obviously pleased that his work represented exactly what he felt. She glanced at Pearl. They both knew that getting Girard to open up was Pearl's task. The two women were a team. Francois put her arm around Girard and kissed him on the cheek. "The details in these are wonderful, and the application of the colors on the face has a knowing touch, Girard. These should be mounted on some type background, maybe burlap, and hung on the Wall." Pearl knew that Girard, lousy mood and all, would enjoy the rest of the day.

During the next hour, Francois chatted with three students, interpreted their work, read and expressed the emotions presented, complimented all, some more than others. On Jean Claude's differential, she picked up that he had cleverly devised a method to mix and apply the secondary color for the bolt heads based upon which stripe they were in. That was why Pearl had not recognized the odd colors.

Natti, accompanied by Father Mike, arrived with fresh coffee, chilled green coconuts filled with coconut milk for each student, and a large batch of homemade cinnamon cookies topped with toasted almonds. Moland, unnecessarily supported by a serpent-shaped ebony walking cane, seemed to limp in. He timed his visit perfectly, just as Natti, and everyone else, expected.

After the half-hour break, Natti picked up the empties and left, leaving most of the cookies behind. Moland, making it known that he wanted more, followed her into the kitchen. Father Mike attentively lingered in the background while Francois resumed counseling. The pile of cookies quickly disappeared. Flies and two sparrows zeroed in on the crumbs.

Francois reviewed the remaining students' works, saving Michelette's until last. The artist stood several feet from the charcoal and carefully studied it. Moisture appeared in her eyes. She took the paint-smeared kerchief dangling from her hip pocket, wiped each cheek, then asked, "Are you going to put this on the wall?"

"No," Michelette responded. "I just felt this. It helped me a lot. I'll probably rub it out and use the canvas again."

"Well then, let me show you something. Anyone have a pencil with an eraser?"

Father Mike handed her one. The artist, using the eraser as an instrument rather than an eradicator, smeared the charcoal on several women's faces, created shadows beneath the trees, made impressions of songbirds on some tree limbs, and accentuated the obese bodies on the plantation owners' caricatures. "Notice how these little touches add a surrealistic mood to the drawing?" she asked. "Just a technique, a refinement."

"Yes," Michelette replied, "I see, but a songbird represents something good. This drawing wasn't meant to be good. It helped me get rid of my bad feelings."

"That's obvious, but it also shows the good you see. The drawing itself is admirable, but the harvesting shown in this manner represents good or plenty." She pointed to the woman ascending into heaven. "Even this representation of death has good in it. Death is real, and the woman's soul is spending eternity in Ginen," she glanced at Father Mike, "or Heaven, not in hell, which says you saw all the good in this woman or, perhaps, in women in general." She turned and spoke to the group. "All of you must recognize that good and bad exist in all things and all people. This drawing magnificently represents their simultaneous existence." She paused. "It also represents love and hate." She pointed to the women and babies. "These women love their children. That's up the scale—the second level of love—and shows in the faces of all the women and some of the men." She paused, then pointed to the owners' caricatures. "This obviously depicts that the plantation owners are despised—hated. Love and hate are both real emotions—just like good and evil. They exist. Side by side."

"I didn't feel any love," Michelette responded.

21

"You may not have felt love, but this drawing shows that you're full of it. It's a wonderful piece."

This was why Pearl enjoyed Francois's visits. She related ideas and concepts in a manner few could. The notion of good and bad and love and hate existing in all humans would be fodder for thought, discussion, and learning for some time to come.

Francois handed the pencil back to Father Mike. "What do you think?"

"The drawing is wonderful."

"That's not to what I was referring." An impish smile spread across her face.

"I know," Father Mike said, returning the smile. "We'll talk about that some evening."

"You're on. Now I have to go." She hugged each student, bid good-bye over her shoulder, and left as confidently as she had come. In just over three short hours, the artist had spread insight and left all the students feeling better about themselves. Even troubled Girard smiled and lifted his oversized hand to wave.

* * *

After school, Moland, as he often did, drew water for Michelette and one other student. She pulled from her backpack a firm, twisted piece of material the shape of a large donut and placed it on her head, then lifted the water-filled jug and positioned it so its weight was properly distributed on the donut. "Thank you. This should last until Monday. Maybe we'll get some rain."

"Would you like a ride partway?" Moland asked, knowing that her home was about an hour's walk.

Michelette's bright eyes gave him his answer before her mouth did. "I don't want to cause any trouble."

"No trouble." He turned to the other student. "How about you?"

The tall, almost white boy with large brown splotches on his face smiled. "I have my bicycle and tow wagon. Thank you anyway."

"I have a few things to do," Moland told Michelette, "then I'll take you as far as your path. Put the water in the back of the truck and have a seat."

"Thank you."

Moland finished his chores. As they drove away, he asked, "How's Mrs. Johnson's gift coming?"

"It's finished," Michelette answered. "It's at Francois's. Do you think Mrs. Johnson knows about the party?"

"I don't think she has a clue."

The staff and students were planning a surprise third anniversary party for Pearl, the only lay teacher who had lasted more than two years. Everyone was looking forward to it, not that many Haitians had to have a reason to party on any given Saturday night. Sister Marie was handling all the proper details while Moland and Father Mike unofficially made the improper arrangements.

Horús Esprit (Moland) Gúyon

The next afternoon, Pearl, waiting under the carport in front of Primal Hall, watched as Michelette walked up carrying her canvas. "Are you going to carry that all the way home?"

"No, ma'am. I'm taking it as far as Francois's. After I help her a bit, she'll drive me to the path."

"You go over to her place a lot, don't you?"

"Yes, ma'am. I do lots of odds and ends." She balanced the edge of the canvas on the toe of her shoe. "I'm learning to mix paints and varnishes, and I stretch canvases and things like that, but mostly I just watch her work and clean up. And we talk a lot." She hesitated, pensively looked down, and twicked a shell with her foot. "I wish Mama liked her more."

Pearl raised her eyebrows. "What do you mean?"

"Mama thinks Francois's bad for me. We have words about it, and Francois feels bad that Mama doesn't like for me to be over there."

This was more information than Pearl was prepared for. Francois did have a unique lifestyle and independent personality. She'd heard all about the artist's nonconforming activities from Sisters Marie and Ester and could understand why a parent might be concerned. "Then why do you go?"

Patting herself, Michelette blurted, "When I hurt in here, I really need somebody to talk to. Francois is the only one that really understands."

Something was troubling the beautiful girl. "Does your mother know you go there as often as you do?"

"I don't tell her cause I don't want to hurt her, but, if she asks, I don't lie. Mama works all the time. She knows she can't keep me from going by there. And it's almost on the way home. I don't know why Mama doesn't like her. Says she's a wicked woman." She pointed to Pearl's overnight bag. "You going away?"

As Pearl finished explaining, Moland, driving the school's blue seven-year-old Honda king-cab pickup, drove up. "Moland is driving me. Can we drop you?"

"Right now I'd as soon walk," Michelette replied, lifting the big canvas. "Besides, I don't think we could get this frame in the truck. Thanks for the talk."

"You're welcome." Pearl held the gate for Michelette. "And if you ever feel the need to talk some more, please come see me."

The young Haitian looked at her and smiled. "Thanks. I might."

Pearl turned to Moland, who had parked the truck and started to get out. "Father Mike got called out and has the Toyota." She was referring to the school's other vehicle, a five-year-old Corolla. "We'll have to take this." She patted the truck's cab.

"Fine," Moland replied as Pearl put her bag behind the seat. "I prefer it anyway cause I've got to stop by my place, and the car scrapes bottom."

Every time Moland carried anyone anywhere, it seemed as if he had to stop by his place to pick up something. After bouncing and grunting over a twisting, rock-strewn excuse of a road for fifteen minutes, they stopped beside his white adobe, corrugated tin roofed cottage. He said he'd be right out. He left the engine running and air conditioning on.

25

Pearl always enjoyed sticking her head in the rustic cabin. This was where she, Father Mike, Moland, usually Francois, and sometimes Georges, the artist's longtime boyfriend, had many long discussions, which, unlike most conversations, seldom turned to sexual innuendoes. "I better take a trip down the path," Pearl said, referring to the shell walkway that led from the cabin's back door to the palm-frond chickee that served as his outhouse.

The cottage's one room was large and had a high, open rafter ceiling. A light gray concrete floor surrounded a six-foot square hardwood center that Moland called his dancing floor. Along one completely windowless wall he had built a seven-shelf bookcase. Concrete blocks supported the thick, roughhewn planks, and neatly arranged books filled the shelves. Two wooden chairs sat in front of the bookshelf. Near another wall was an old canvas cot with neatly folded blue muslin sheets at the foot and two thick yellow pillows at the head. Stacks of books on each side served as bedside stands. Several chairs sat next to the third wall. His only table—a large, somewhat rectangular slab of solid mahogany supported by four more stacks of books, sat along a wall under a window. His wardrobe hung on a shiny horizontal piece of copper tubing in the corner between the cot and table. The four starched and pressed shirts, three pairs of trousers with sharp creases, one suit, one tie, and an all-weather jacket hung equally spaced. A small stack of underwear, several pairs of socks, some work pants, and T-shirts lay methodically stacked on the corner shelf above his wardrobe. On the floor beneath, he kept a pair of polished dress shoes, clean work boots, and sandals.

What caught most people by surprise on their first visit was in the opposite corner—a polished, elegantly unpretentious altar and kneeling stool. A bonsai tree about the size of a small table lamp sat on the altar. Above the tree, suspended from a spider-web-thin black wire, hung a baseball size, hand-carved wooden globe. A small hollow container with water and floating flower petals sat on one side of the tree, and on the other, in a similar container, a small terrarium. Red candles in brass holders on each edge of the altar completed its ensemble. A small hand carving on the right-hand wall said, "BONDYE BON." Beneath this Creole saying, in smaller letters, were the words, "God is Good." Only when visitors learned that Moland was a Houngan—a Vodoun priest—did they understand the altar and dance floor.

Pearl stepped out the rear door. An open, two hearth fireplace situated so Moland could observe it from the window over the table sat beside the path. A heavy iron grille sat on one hearth, on the other a stainless steel distillation pot and coil. Glass containers, in descending order, neatly lined the two shelves beside the distillation unit, or still, as the setup is more commonly called. Empty containers occupied the upper shelf; those on the lower rack were filled with a clear liquid which Moland referred to as heavy water or nectar of the gods, but it's more commonly known as taffia or clarin. Americans, particularly Southerners, tended to call it cane moonshine or Haitian white lightning. Moland, saying it was necessary to assure proper quality, always made his own.

As Pearl returned from the end of the path, Moland selected a small unsealed bottle and poured a bit in two small shot glasses. "We should make sure this hasn't gone bad, right?"

"Of course," Pearl replied. Following Moland's example, she chugged her shot, then faked a wheeze, and patted herself on the chest. "Whew! That hasn't gone bad."

Pearl got along well with Moland. Much better than the nuns. She had grown to respect the old fellow. When she first met him, she assumed that he was a poverty-stricken Haitian struggling to make ends meet. Now she placed him near the top of her Most Unforgettable People list. He once said, during one of their many sessions, that he was lucky to be as wealthy as he was. With a roof over his head, all he wanted to eat and drink, and his books, what else could a man ask for? The mission that he had set for his life, he always said, was to help others learn to share the treasures that our Gods have given us. Unfortunately, according to the shaman, most people lived their lives foolishly chasing the wind when they should pass into transcendence and enjoy the ever-present abundant surroundings. He was satisfied with his place in the universe, a contentment that Pearl envied. She adored the old priest and felt that he truly respected her.

"I'll take another." She indicated a wee bit with her fingers.

"It's a special brew." He winked. "This batch will bring you magic." A mischievous smile lit his craggy face as she downed the second shot. "It'll free up your thinking just a bit. Now, let's hit the road." He handed Pearl the gallon of spirits. "Please take this for me. I have some more things to get."

"And if we run out of gas," she added, taking the jug, "we can use this."

He chuckled and, on the way through the cabin, gathered up several books, his one suit, and the pair of dress shoes. He hung the suit along the back of the cab then used the books and shoes to brace the spirits. Satisfied, they began the two-and-a-half hour journey to la Villa Creole.

Michelette

Francois cleaned brushes at a round flamingo-pink clay table inlaid with aqua ceramic marine figurines. She usually left the task for Michelette but, today, yesterday, and the day before, her mind had wandered often to Georges so she resorted to doing something that would not require mental effort. Frequently she would stare longingly over the Gulf of Gonave, hoping for a glimpse of one of her lover's fishing schooners.

The yellow adobe buildings of La Petite, her compound, were more than two hundred years old and originally served as the house and barn for the commandeur of an aloe plantation. One of the estate's original clay boiling pits, the compound's centerpiece, sat centered between the structures. Another piece of the original plantation, the cistern, almost hidden by a large bougainvillea, sat shaded by an extension of the carport roof, a small pump and pressure tank beside it.

Francois lived in the commandeur's original quarters, which had two large rooms. When she renovated, she removed two walls facing the water and installed wall-to-wall sliding glass doors and added a bathroom with a ceramic tile bathtub, a separate spacious shower, a bidet, and standard water closet. Her studio, about twice the size of her house, was formerly the plantation's barn and aloe bottling facility. For more light and cross ventilation, she had added jalousie windows around the perimeter near the old roofline. Both buildings had matching white concrete tile roofs.

The shadows cast by the afternoon sun told her that Michelette would be arriving soon. At that precise moment, the gong at the front gate upset the serene setting. Francois knew it was Michelette and could tell from the strength of the gong's tone that the youngster was upset about something. She lifted the electronic sender/receiver from her waistband. "Yes?"

"It's me."

Francois pressed a red button on the sender and listened as the security gate squeaked open, paused, squealed, and clicked shut, then called, "I'm at the table."

Michelette came around the corner, leaned her canvas against Francois's Suzuki parked under the carport behind the cistern, tossed her backpack into the car, and walked over.

"There's some lemonade in the refrigerator. Help yourself."

Michelette disappeared through the side door, then called, "Want some?"

"I have some. Thanks anyway."

Michelette strolled out, sat opposite Francois, picked up two brushes and dipped them into the pan of initial cleanser, an almost black liquid. "Looks like you've already cleaned most of them."

"I haven't been in the mood for serious painting for the last couple of days. Today was especially bad. How are things at school?"

"Fine," Michelette replied.

Francois, who had been looking at the final rinse, rolled her eyes up and looked at the girl. "What's bothering you?"

"How did you know something was bothering me?"

"Some people say I can see beyond." Francois did not take her eyes off Michelette. "What's up?"

"Well, this is Friday night."

"Oh. The test?"

"Yes!" She stabbed a brush into the final rinse. "Why does she do it?"

Francois, the adult, knew she could only encourage the child to find her own path through the forest of religious dogma and tradition. She remembered her own mother's testing, but it wasn't something to discuss with Michelette, not at this point anyway. At bedtime every Saturday night, Francois's mother tested the artist's virginity to see if she had anything to confess at mass. Francois tried to get her mother to stop but couldn't, and recalled plotting a way to finally put a stop to the inquisitive, humiliating finger. It was the weekend of her eleventh birthday. Francois had dipped a medium green banana in coconut cooking oil, wrapped it in a banana tree leaf, and sneaked it into her bedroom. She recalled her minor physical discomfort and jubilant emotional satisfaction as she used the banana to break her own hymen. Knowing what would soon come, she left the banana in place and pulled the sheet over herself.

On schedule, her mother, a very fat African, waddled in, the floor planks squealing with each heavy step, and, as always, told her rebellious daughter to spread her legs. Francois obeyed and smiled as she recalled her mother's stout hand pulling back the cover. The big woman took one look at the protruding fruit, clasped her fat cheeks with both hands, and screamed. Her eyes blossomed, rolled up, and the woman fainted dead away. With a thunderous quake, she smashed the fragile bed. She was so heavy the family let her lie until she revived. It was more than two weeks before she spoke to Francois, and then only in short, cursory tones. But the artist never again had to suffer through the mortifying test. That had been her first step on her path through the forest of independence. Michelette had to find her own path.

"The tests are a mother's way to confirm virginity, to assure that their daughters are not sexually active until they are matched," Francois heard herself saying. "Original beliefs of the ancients were that we at one time lived in Ginen, a pure, clean environment where we existed amongst that which bestowed us. Now we live in a devastated, deforested, and, some say, deflowered condition. Testing, according to folktale, is a ritual from that tradition, one that encourages young women to stay chaste until the proper time to give another human a chance at an undefiled life."

"But all it says to me is that she doesn't trust me," Michelette said. "She says that she does, and says that it's a way to prove to a man that I don't have the plague, and to tell the boys that I can't do what they want me to do because my mother will find out."

"Well, to some degree, she's right. And with the AIDS scourge running amuck, it would be a sign of being free." *(God,)* she thought, *(I'm beginning to sound like a mother.)*

"I just tell boys no, that I don't want to. I don't need any more reason than that. Besides, Mrs. Johnson says girls can break their hymens playing, you know, doing things like climbing trees and running and jumping, and I used to do that all the time, but I quit because of the stupid test." She stopped for a moment. "And if a man can't take my word that I'm clean, then he won't be the one for me!"

Francois was hearing herself almost twenty years before. "Do you use a tampon?"

"I'm scared to. Mrs. Johnson says they can cause separation. Besides, we can't afford them, and I don't think Mama would allow it anyway. But why doesn't she just trust me?"

"It isn't a matter of trust, Mikey," Francois said, recalling her own reputation. "Often perception is involved, especially with us women." She knew rumors abounded about her but was comfortable knowing that Georges, her soul mate of nine years, was the only man with whom she had ever been. Her mind flitted from Georges, who hadn't visited in more than

33

two weeks, to the times after her final testing when an oiled banana served to relieve massive amounts of tension. She withheld a smile. "Not only is your mother doing what she thinks is best for you, she's also trying to assure that other people's perception is as it should be. Someday you might understand her concern and that she is only trying, in the way of the ancients, to protect you."

La Villa Creole

Pearl and Moland made good time along Route One, the main highway between St. Marc and Port-au-Prince. But, as expected, just before crossing the Grise River, traffic increased significantly. Moland's heavy water must have worked because Pearl buried herself deep in thought. In heavy traffic, they crept to the intersection with the Boulevard du Fifteen October. Most of the traffic continued toward Port-au-Prince, but they turned up the road toward Freres. There, in this hillside community, the traffic stopped. "It's still the fastest way," Moland said, glancing over. "Lock your door."

The comment startled Pearl from her thoughts. She slammed the lock down.

Massive quantities of paper, plastic bottles, pieces of tires, and other junk littered the roadway, a far cry from the neat environment of St. Jude's.

"What's bothering you?" Moland asked. "You've been unusually quiet. You're normally so excited about seeing Wayne that you chatter like Sister Joan."

He moved to the middle of the road to avoid a
stripped-down junk car crowding the right-of-way.

"I'm sorry. I was thinking about Francois's
comments." She glanced up at the clouds. "Looks like
we're gonna get some rain."

"What did Franny have to say when I wasn't
there?"

As the traffic crept through Freres, Pearl explained
Francois's comments about Michelette's drawing.
Pearl added that, in all her years, she had not bothered
giving too much thought about good and evil, love and
hate. She was too busy being. Being a dutiful wife.
Being a dedicated mother. Being a dependable teacher.
Being a good churchgoer. Being attendant to her social
duties. She said that she seemed to recollect that a
woman's calling was preordained—be all things to all
people. Except to herself, which, she was told, was
selfish.

A veil of moisture descended from the dark clouds.
Moland switched on the windshield wipers, then
fussed at the dirty streaks they caused. He pushed the
windshield washer button. It spat a few drops. "Come
on. I fixed you last week." He pressed twice more.
Finally, a thin mist spewed over the glass. "Finally!"
He sighed, then glanced at Pearl. "Franny's right.
Good. Evil. Love. Hate. All exist in each of us. Which
ones dominate is the key." The rain fell harder. "Hope
we get some of this down on the flats." The traffic
slowed even more. "Damn slippery roads," he
mumbled. After two prolonged traffic holds and a near
miss with a skidding motorcycle, they turned off the
main road. "Almost there."

"This may sound stupid," Pearl said, "particularly for someone my age, but I'm not sure I have ever really truly loved anyone, much less God."

In a drizzle, they pulled under la Villa Creole's canopy. "That's neither stupid nor childish, regardless of age. How about your children?"

"Well, of course I love them."

"Then you love God. But love is not simple. Perhaps sometime, with Father Mike and a little mind-broadening elixir," he reached back and patted the jug, "we'll pursue the subject at length. Need help with your bag?"

"No, thanks. And there are some cars behind us. See you here Monday between ten and noon. Thanks for the ride." She quickly slipped from the truck.

Weighing Moland's comments, she strolled through the covered, quarry-stone entrance, and across the polished, natural stone tile floor. The majestic maroon, yellow, and pink bougainvilleas growing between the alabaster white arches of the open-air lobby grabbed her attention. A man in a white Panama hat hurried past and up to the check-in counter, set his computer case on the floor, and asked for his key and messages.

Pearl spotted Wayne sitting at a table near the end of the pool sipping a red punch from a tall glass. He waved and rose. She smiled, returned the gesture, then walked up two steps to the shiny hardwood floor surrounding the counter. She glanced to see if Wayne was near, stumbled over the computer case, dropped her overnight bag, and fell against the computer owner's sturdy six-foot frame; he, with apparent ease, steadied her.

"Oh, I'm sorry," she exclaimed, righting herself. She felt her face flush, like the oncoming of a hot flash. She knew she was blushing. "I'm so embarrassed."

"It's not your fault," he said. "I should be more careful where I set the case. Are you okay?" With his foot, he moved his computer closer to the counter.

"My ego's bruised." She straightened her dress.

Wayne, looking more like a beach bum than a marine biologist, reached the scene and put his arm around her. "Your mother just made a fool of herself." The two were about the same height.

"I don't think so," the gentleman replied, lifting the computer and sliding the strap over his shoulder. "It was my fault and could have turned out much more serious. Next time I'll make sure the case isn't where someone could trip." He took his key and messages from the counter. "Please accept my apologies. I hope you enjoy the evening." He disappeared around the corner before she could reply.

Pétionville

Robert Lane (Bob) Turner

Bob Turner, in Haiti to support government authorities with the renovation of the University Hospital's emergency room and intensive care unit, walked briskly down the main corridor to the passageway leading to his room. He had made many trips to Haiti, stayed at homes of friends, and in several hotels. He preferred private homes but, due to Carnival, when Haitian families usually get together, he chose not to impose. He managed to get Room D, which he considered the Creole's coziest.

Bob considered the picturesque, multilevel complex, nestled into one of the many hillsides of surrounding Port-au-Prince, to be the best hotel in Haiti. It was comfortable, safe, convenient to the hospital, near Pétionville's art center, had a sizable swimming pool, and access to several tennis courts. A unique poolside cocktail lounge and fashionable dining room specializing in gourmet Haitian and French cuisine completed the hotel's friendly ambiance.

The main corridor overlooked the split-level combination lounge/dining room, the lower level of which melded with the pool deck. Thick white columns and mahogany railings separated the corridor and dining areas. Bob paused momentarily at the large, fresh floral arrangement sitting on the ledge between columns, fingered one of the dozen or more bright red anthuriums that intermingled with deep green philodendron leaves, then glanced at the pool and debated whether or not to change into his swim trunks. Even in the misting rain, joining the several swimmers seemed enticing. He glanced at his University of Florida Gator watch, a Father's Day gift from his children several years before. Undecided, he opened the door to his room, set his hat on top of the television, dumped the computer on the bed, turned on the air conditioning, and read the first of his four messages. Franck St. Fleur, a Haitian professional engineer with whom Bob worked and had stayed several times, said that he and Presley would get to the lounge about seven. In Haiti, because of the traffic and road conditions, seven meant anywhere between six and eight. Franck had, in order to finalize an important Rotary International humanitarian aid project, arranged a meeting with Presley Dumas, president of the Rotary Club of Port-au-Prince. Bob glanced again at his watch. Plenty of time to shower, shave, and swim.

The other messages were from his three children. Marcia, one of the twenty-two-year-old twins, was a mathematician in California and the most long-winded of the trio. She never cut her dad, or anyone else, any slack. Her note read "Eight to ten Saturday, PDT' followed by her number and the comment, "'cause I know the second thing to go is memory and don't get uptight if a man answers." Bob smiled. She knew he had memorized all their numbers, and he, as well as her two brothers, encouraged Marcia to accept the teaching fellowship at Stanford to pursue a master's, not men. The males in the family also knew that she listened but merrily danced through life to her own music.

Marc, the older twin by four minutes and a first-year high school band director in Arcadia, Florida, suggested a call between nine and ten. Harry, a twenty-four-year-old Exxon engineer-in-training in Houston, just said don't call too early Saturday, which meant not before ten. All three knew that this would be a difficult weekend for their father. Two years ago tomorrow, with Bob sitting at bedside holding her hand, Sarah, his high school sweetheart, wife since midway through college, spiritual soul mate, and mother of his children, succumbed to the rapid onslaught of ovarian cancer. Even though her death had been expected, and was known to be a physical relief, the final exhale ended her wonderful circle of life and began his period of aloneness.

He slipped into his Tommy Bahama bathing trunks, a reminder of his last birthday celebrated in the Virgin Islands seven months back. The kids had surprised him with a trip to St. Thomas. He hadn't particularly wanted to be by himself, but they had really wanted to do something special. To make them feel good, he had chosen to keep quiet and accept their generosity. He recalled how lonesome he had been on the crowded flight from Miami to St. Thomas, only to be overjoyed when Marcia and Marc, and Harry and his new wife, Jody, surprised him at the airport.

Bob went to the pool by way of the rear garden. When he reached the deck, he hung his towel over a sheltered rack, kicked off his Birkenstocks, dove in, and swam the length of the pool and back underwater. As he hung on the edge of the sheltered end catching his breath, Thom, one of the waiters, dressed in formal dinner wear, walked up.

"Mr. Turner, would you like your Barbancourt Reserve rum punch?"

"Please, Thom. Thank you."

"My pleasure, sir." He turned and smartly strode away.

As Bob breathlessly stroked his fourth lap, he saw Thom spread a large white napkin at the edge of the pool and set upon it a tall drink and a familiar glass chalice containing roasted peanuts and banana chips. He swam to the edge, drew a sip of punch through the reed straw, closed his eyes, and allowed his taste buds the luxury of bathing in the ecstasy of the rich Barbancourt drink. When he lifted his eyelids, he saw a pair of brown, slightly damp wingtips. He followed the blue trousers up to a striped blue-on-white short-sleeve shirt into the familiar chocolate face of Franck St. Fleur. "You're early."

"I wanted to be here before Presley."

Bob hoisted himself from the pool, stepped away from the white cloth, and got his towel. Thom approached. "Franck, order something. I'll go in, change, and join you at a table."

"No hurry." Franck turned to the waiter. "Presidenté, please."

"Yes, sir. Mr. Turner, may I take your drink to the refrigerator?"

"No, Thom," Bob said, reaching down and picking up the tall glass, "I'll take it with me. When you see me at the table, please bring another."

"Yes, sir." Thom turned and motioned for the busboy, who hurried over and picked up the white cloth and chalice.

Michelette's Neighborhood

Francois drove Michelette along the pothole-ridden road that roughly followed the coast to her well-worn path. Michelette, knowing what faced her later that evening, reluctantly got out of the car. She thanked Francois for the ride and for promising to clean the canvas and disassemble the frame so it could be brought home next time. Francois started to make a U-turn, but a United Nations' open-topped humvee, carrying three soldiers, rounded the bend up ahead. Wary, Michelette stood close to Francois's door. As the humvee rumbled by, two soldiers waved, and one whistled.

"Some peacekeepers," Francois said. "Pay them no mind." When the humvee's dust settled, Francois wheeled the Suzuki around and drove away.

When the weather was bad, which was almost never, Francois, or someone else, would usually drive Michelette all the way home, but the path really twisted and turned so badly it was easier, and about as fast, to walk. As she strolled down the familiar trail between a small grove of coconut palms and a large sugarcane field, a cane toad hopped into and quickly out of her way. She walked under some mango trees, and, trying to develop a positive attitude toward the upcoming virginal test, paused and listened to the music of the leaves, orchestrated by a gentle breeze and accompanied by chirping sparrows and cardinals. She understood her mother's love and concern. Maybe she didn't want to do it as bad as Michelette didn't want it done. Maybe Francois was right. Maybe her mother was following some ancient instinct she couldn't help.

"Hey, Michelette!" called the familiar, expectant voice of her only lifelong playmate.

"What do you want, Eduardo?" He almost always waited for her to come home from school.

The gangly boy with brownish-blond skin and long, tangled black hair dropped from a mango tree near the path and trotted over. "Yo mama's not home yet, and yo late."

"I'm glad." She picked up her pace. "Francois and I talked a long time. And I still have to weed the beans, or I'll be in lots of trouble." As long as she could remember, her mother had kept two gardens, one of various vegetables, and another strictly for beans. Beans, her mother always said, were necessary for good development, something she didn't have growing up, but swore that her daughter would. When Michelette got old enough, keeping the gardens free of weeds became her responsibility.

The teenagers hurried through the grove. He was just a little older than she, lived nearby, and their mothers were friends. His father, like Michelette's, had disappeared trying to get to the United States. He was kind of like a brother that Michelette imagined the two that died before their first birthday would have been. But in the past two years he had changed. Being a little slow in the brain, he had quit school and spent most of his time working the cane fields, fishing along the coast, and helping his mother make charcoal. He and Michelette had had a lot of fun together when they were little. Growing apart saddened her.

"Wha'd you talk about?" he asked.

"Art, mostly." She never said anything to him about being tested. They used to talk a lot. But recently he did most of the talking and had become somewhat impulsive. His strange behavior had started just before he quit school, right after he had confided in her that he had started "feeling funny down there," referring to his groin.

"You always drew good pictures. Remember when you painted faces on my back? Our mamas had fits." He slapped a mosquito that had landed on his shoulder.

She nodded and laughed, absentmindedly blowing gnats away from her face. She had used some oils to paint three clown faces on his back. They'd had lots of good times, and she still liked it when he waited and walked home with her. She tried to get him to go back to school, but he wouldn't, saying that he didn't need schoolin' to work the cane and fish.

She noticed that he had lost some of his enthusiasm. One problem continued to come up that made her feel uncomfortable. For more than a year now, he frequently asked her to "play man and woman" meaning to let him put his thing between the fork in her legs. She always said no and, most often, that was that. But once in a while he would persist, saying that everybody does it. Two times in recent weeks he went so far as to show her his stiff member. She had seen it many times when he relieved himself, just as he had seen her doing the same thing. But that had been a long time ago. Stiff, it was a lot bigger than she could ever imagine. The last time, he actually pulled his pants down and tried to get her to touch it. Curiosity had tinged her mind, but she said no. He pouted, but only for a few minutes.

"Want me to hep you pull weeds?"

His offer surprised her because he hadn't been all that considerate since he pulled his pants down. He used to always be thoughtful but recently seemed to be all mixed up. It was nice to see the familiar side again. "I'd like that."

Dinner at La Villa Creole

Pearl, thankful for the Villa's complimentary bath oil, shampoo, and conditioner, slouched indulgently in a tub of fragrant warm water, her head tingling from the lather. She had agreed to meet Wayne in the dining room in a Haitian hour. It had been three months since his last visit, hence three months since she had savored a luxurious, gratifying warm bath. Reluctantly, using the flexible spray head, she finished her hair, rinsed, toweled off, and used the room's hair dryer. She ran her fingers through her hair. It hadn't felt so soft and silky since her last stay. She was beginning to feel like a pampered woman.

Picking out what to wear wasn't a problem. She'd only brought one dressy outfit, a rayon and polyester cobalt blue suit with gold buttons and complementary gold shell. She slipped the shell over her head, then stepped into the long flowing split skirt. She leisurely applied her makeup, taking particular care to cover the scar, checked and straightened her hair, then stepped back from the mirror. Patting her hips, she mumbled, "Better watch those fried bananas." Satisfied, she slipped on a pair of gold low heels, picked up her matching bag and jacket, and walked down to the main level, through the garden, to the Grand Corridor. The canopied walkway protected her hair from the misting rain.

As she walked beside the arches, she spotted Wayne at a sheltered table near the pool. Its surface resembled frosted glass because of the light, steady drizzle. A gentle breeze drifted through the area, enhanced by the overhead fans. Chilled, she slipped on her jacket as she walked down the stairs leading to the dining terraces. Dodging waiters and slipping sideways between diners and chairs, she wove her way across the slate floor and took her place at the small round table.

"You look great, Mom, but I can't believe you have a jacket on. I'm a little warm. I chose this table to catch all the wind possible."

"I'm sure it's just the chill before the meltdown. I imagine I'll be shedding it pretty soon." She moved the fresh-cut orange-and-blue bird of paradise to one side so she could see her son's face. "Did Rose get you the estrogen?" she asked, referring to a promise her sister had made by e-mail.

Wayne reached into a pocket of his green and white guayabera and handed her a bottle of Premarin. "I have five more in the room."

"Thanks." She opened the bottle, placed a capsule in her mouth, and chased it with a sip of Wayne's water. "Unfortunately it will take a couple of weeks before they take full effect. How is Rose?" She slipped the bottle into her purse.

"Fine. She sends her best and said to tell you she's planning on coming down sometime within the next two months. She'll let you know as soon as she can arrange her vacation. Care for a drink?"

"I'd like that."

Wayne motioned for the waiter, who was tending a table of five. "The place is packed so service'll be slow."

"I'm in no hurry. The bath was wonderful. Besides, it gives us time to catch up. How's the job going? Been what now? A year?"

"Almost two, and it's great. Bureaucracies like Natural Resources can get somewhat frustrating, but I enjoy Pennekamp." He was referring to John Pennekamp Coral Reef State Park at Key Largo, Florida, where he was the staff biologist. "I still look forward to going to work every day, and if I play my cards right, I suspect I'll be there as long as I want."

"Do you hear anything from Beverly?"

"She sends her regards. She's pretty well settled into the school and new apartment in Flagstaff."

"Is she seeing anyone?"

"I don't think so, but she probably wouldn't say if she was."

"Do you have a recent picture? The last one I have was at her graduation. How does she look?" Pearl knew he had one. He was always considerate, especially during the rough times. He had his father's broad shoulders, and his work kept him dark and handsome. Too bad he wasn't tall along with it.

"She's fine, Mom." He handed her an envelope. "Here's some snapshots from when she was down this past summer."

The waiter approached. "May I get you something from the bar?"

"Mango tea, please," Pearl replied.

"And you, sir?"

Wayne motioned to his glass.

"Are you ready to order?" the waiter asked.

Pearl patted the menu lying on her place mat. "I haven't even looked at it. Please give us a few minutes."

"Thank you, ma'am." The waiter turned and walked away.

Pearl thumbed through the photos. "She does look good, doesn't she? Can I keep these?"

"Yes to both." He paused. "Mom, I feel like I'm in the middle here."

"I know." She reached across the table and covered her hand with his. "You're a prince." She withdrew her hand. "For some reason, we just can't communicate. I've tried every way I know how to get through. Any suggestions?"

"I know she loves you. It's just that . . . "

"She can't understand why I stayed with Ted all those years. She feels that I was prostituting myself."

"That, along with why you haven't agreed to the divorce."

"Both of you know why. Is she still not speaking to her father?"

"Won't even talk about him, much less to him! See, that's the type of thing that makes me uncomfortable. I feel like a snitch." What he didn't tell his mother was that Sister Ester had contacted him about Pearl's surprise anniversary party and asked if he could arrange to bring Beverly. Also, could he bring some of Pearl's favorite music? This particular weekend visit came about because of his mother's desperate call for estrogen. But this trip actually served three purposes. The obvious was to bring the medicine, which, because of Haitian law, couldn't be shipped in. Second, by sheer coincidence, it would serve as a diversion so Pearl would not suspect anything. But more important than both, Wayne wanted Beverly's visit not to end in yet another confrontation. He had had to work hard to convince his sister to make the trip. In the two-hour-long phone conversation with her, he discovered that he didn't know his mother's favorite music, but Bev did and had agreed to bring along several CDs.

"As a mother, how do you think I feel? I can't communicate with my own daughter. I know I made mistakes. We all do. But one thing a person never gets is a second chance to be a parent to the same child." She felt a hot flash coming on and shifted to pull off her jacket. She had difficulty with the initial move and,

Jim Henry

just as she was about to rise from her chair, someone behind her grasped the collar, stabilizing the garment. She slipped her arm from the sleeve and looked up into a man's hazel eyes. "Thank you."

"You're welcome," he replied. "Have a nice dinner."

She watched the good Samaritan as he shook hands with one of the men at the next table and sat, his back to her. She leaned slightly toward Wayne and whispered, "That's the same man with whom I had the accident at the front desk. I don't think he recognized me, thank goodness. He'd probably think I was a helpless klutz."

Wayne smiled. "Why would he recognize you? You look much better than when you checked in."

"Gee, thanks a lot. Did I look that bad?"

"That was supposed to be a compliment, Mom," Wayne said, chuckling. "We men can't win. What I meant was that when you first came in you looked like you used to look on Fridays after a hard week at school; you know, kinda like you'd been through the grinder."

"That doesn't get your foot out of your mouth, you know." Pearl removed a dainty folding fan from her evening bag.

"Trust me, Mom. You look great." He paused. An impish grin crossed his face. "Now anyway!"

Pearl unfolded the fan and, using short, rapid strokes, tried to cool her hot, sweaty face. Wayne's grin widened. "What? Is my eye shadow running or something?"

"The way you're fanning," he said, raising a hand and flapping it, "reminds me of the wings of a hovering hummingbird or kingfisher."

"Before I was freezing. Now I'm roasting." She picked up the two-page menu. "Let's see what's on the menu."

The Rotary Project

Bob shook hands with Presley Dumas, an elegantly dressed Haitian several inches shorter than he. "Good to see you again, Pres. I enjoyed visiting your club Monday evening." The three men settled in their chairs as the waiter walked up and set a tall rum punch in front of Bob.

"Would you gentlemen care for an appetizer?" Thom asked. They all shook their heads. "I'll be back in a few minutes."

On Bob's second trip to Haiti almost two years before, Franck, knowing Bob was a Rotarian and conscientious about his attendance record, had arranged for him to make up missed meetings at the Rotary Club of Port-au-Prince. Through this initial contact, Bob's and Presley's respective clubs ultimately applied to Rotary International for a matching Humanitarian Grant to drill a well and install a generator and switchgear, the first steps toward making a clinic Franck had been working with near St. Marc, recently renamed the Rotary Clinic, a high-quality primary-care facility. Bob's club furnished a large portion of the funds, Presley's club supplied some money, project administration, and in-kind services, and the Rotary Foundation granted the remainder of the costs. Bob's goal this trip, along with University Hospital duties, was to attend the dedication and issue final approval for funds disbursement, and to observe the ministering of the polio vaccine, a joint project between Rotary and the World Health Organization. His ultimate goal was to work out the logistics to see that the clinic had the necessary medical supplies for the next five years. This clinic was to be the prototype for other primary health care facilities throughout Haiti. A rather ambitious undertaking.

Bob sipped his punch. "I'm looking forward to the dedication. I assume everything has had its trial run?" Presley was an electrical engineer and supervised the generator installation. Bob anticipated the answer.

"Yes," Presley replied. "Good flow of water from the well, too, and the generator and transfer switch work fine. My hope is that this is the first of a long line of successful clinics." He paused. "The staff up there is in the process of administering the polio vaccine. Some of our club will be up there helping."

"How about customs?"

"We're still having a little difficulty there," Franck said. "Haiti gets a lot of unusable equipment donated. That means instead of helping, it becomes a problem because we have to get rid of it, which, as you know, is difficult. We're overrun with trash now."

Bob knew this firsthand. He had seen many pieces of cannibalized equipment, medical and otherwise, strewn by the side of the roads due to the lack of organized waste disposal. And most modern medical equipment requires stable, clean electric power, which Haiti normally doesn't have. That was why he pressed for and got a stable electrical system at the Rotary Clinic. With dependable power, the operating-room lights, sterilizers, X-ray equipment, centrifuges, respirators, medical refrigerators, computers, and all other electrical equipment should remain useful.

"We have a group that checks all the equipment before it is sent," Bob said. "Perhaps if we sent a certification along with it?"

"That might help," Presley said, sipping his punch, "but that adds to the paperwork. We're trying to work with them and say that we'll be responsible. I believe they'll buy that, but we have to wait and see."

This was a critical point. The clinic would need examination tables and lights, sterilizers, blood pressure measuring devices, and other primary care items. Additional paperwork strains volunteer services. In addition, they would need to send essential medical supplies like sheets, gauze, tape, disinfectants, Band-Aids, and hypodermic needles. Having these supplies tied up in customs would pose a significant hardship. The advantage of working with local Rotarians was that they usually find a way to cut through this type of problem.

Franck joined in. "As you know, I work with children's homes in the provinces. Two months ago, a six-year-old boy from a home in Grand Anse had a compound fracture of his leg and went to a local clinic. They had no disinfectant, had to use sticks from bushes to make a splint, and rip sheets for bandage, and to tie it up. It took them so long to get him to the University

Hospital that infection had already set in. They had to amputate below the knee."

From the first time Bob came to Haiti, he had admired its citizens for the proud, fiercely independent people they were. They, as a nation, would rather live in freedom under difficult conditions than be obligated to any outside government. They were deeply religious and not particularly judgmental. Organized religion classified the spiritual climate as 90 percent Catholic and 100 percent voodoo.

Early on, he concluded that Haitians want, and have the capability, to solve their own problems. They appreciate outside assistance, but not in return for subservience. The individual citizens, as a whole, did not trust government of any kind. Instead, they depended on one another, starting with the family, then their neighbors, then the village.

The Test

Michelette lay propped in bed supported by a yellowing feather pillow. A threadbare blue sheet covered her naked body. She flipped through the pages of a manila paper pamphlet she had made in Mrs. Johnson's art and literature class. The booklet, bound by a shiny orchid ribbon threaded through notebook holes, contained a collection of Maya Angelou poems. Mrs. Johnson had made copies for each student, who bound the pages together. Throughout the year, she would read one of the poems, lead a discussion about its meaning, then ask each student to draw interpretations in the margins. When Michelette reached her favorite, "I Know Why the Caged Bird Sings," which she knew by heart, she paused and studied it once again, trying to extract additional meaning and strength from it. It was at times like this that she, like the caged bird, longed to be free of the old-fashioned traditions. Flickering shadows cast by the single candle on the mango-crate bedside table made her artistic interpretations leap free from the pages. Was this a sign? She wondered how to open the discussion with her mother.

A scraping noise momentarily diverted her attention. She glanced toward the sound just as a large beetle, its shiny armor reflecting the candlelight, dragged itself over and seem to fall through one of the half-inch openings in the unfinished wood-plank floor just beneath her two blue and white school uniforms and one dressy dress hanging from a cord stretched across one corner of her room. "Good night, Mr.

Beetle," she said. "I wish I could crawl through the crack with you." At least she had wood floors raised off the ground. Eduardo only had a dirt floor.

She tensed at the sound of her mother's footsteps, laid the poetry collection aside, and pulled the flimsy cover up to her chin. Even though the evening was warm, she felt as if she had buried herself under a thin layer of blue ice. The bottom edge of the leather-hinged door to her small bedroom scraped the floor. She shut her eyes and gritted her teeth so hard her jaws ached. Little bumps popped out on her skin. Chills rattled every bone.

"Michelette?" her mother asked.

"Yes, ma'am?" Michelette gazed fearfully into the dark, gentle eyes recessed in her mother's brown-black, wrinkled face. Two missing teeth, one in front on the top and the other off to the side on bottom, helped make her look as if she'd been on earth many more than thirty-one years. Two coarse strands of grey hair snaked through the remaining coal black, thinning hair that clung to her taut scalp. She walked with a slight stoop caused by years of bending over making briquettes. Her sun-shriveled skin seemed glued to her frail bones. She worked hard to assure that, through Michelette's education, sometime in the future life would be better for both of them. This was the dream that kept her trudging year after year. Through compassion, Michelette experienced her mother's fatigue and had promised herself long before that she would not disappoint. Michelette did all of the cooking, laundry, cleaning, and other housework. She would have helped make charcoal, but her mother would not allow it, saying that no daughter of hers would ever have to make briquettes. But there was one major issue between them, and it reared its ugly head every Friday evening.

"Are you ready?"

From deep within, Michelette mustered all the courage she had. She breathed rapidly. Her heart pounded. She had to do it. "Mama?"

"Yes."

Her mother sat on the edge of the bed.

Michelette felt the tears welling up. "Mama." She hesitated. "Do you have to do this?"

A kind smile crossed her mother's face. "Little Flower, a woman is special. She must remain pure until she is married. This is our way."

"But can't you trust me to tell you whether or not I'm pure?"

"Of course, but it isn't a matter of trust." Her mother spoke slowly, as if from memory rather than thought. "It is a matter for the gods. Like the blessing we give before each meal. We thank God for the food he has given us. The test is a blessing of your purity and of the purity of the life you will, in time, have born to you. Besides, if you have remained pure, what is the problem?"

At least her mother was talking about it, which, in itself, relieved Michelette, but her heart still pounded. "I feel like you don't trust me. Besides, it seems to me that if it is a matter for the gods that it would be between me and the gods, not me, you, and the gods." Her lower lip trembled. She knew she had said the wrong thing before it got all the way out of her mouth. Tears flowed from the corners of her eyes.

Her mother's face tightened so hard it seemed that her wrinkles disappeared. "That's that artist feeding you words!"

"Mama . . . "

She was going to say they were her words, not Francois's, but her mother interrupted. "One of these days you will thank me," she snapped. "Many times boys who wanted me to play with them backed off when I told them I'd have to tell my mother. It is for your own good."

"But Mama, I . . . "

"Now look what you've done! I came in here peaceful and now look at me." She sighed deeply and slumped. She looked like she was going to die.

"Mama, I —"

"Michelette, just don't say nothin else!"

Her mother seldom spoke such harsh words. They sat in silence for what seemed like hours. Michelette stared at the shadows dancing on the underside of the tin roof. She felt movement on the bed and heard her mother humming softly. Michelette shifted her eyes from the shadows and watched her mother sway rhythmically. With a smooth, clear voice led by the spirits of the wind, the skeletal woman started chanting an ancient Voduan tale of which Michelette did not understand the meaning. Suddenly, she stopped and took a long, deep breath. With tears rolling down her cheeks, she closed her eyes, resumed a different, very sad, melody, and gently slid her hand beneath the sheets.

Tears poured from Michelette's eyes as the ghosts of tradition crept between her thighs. She sobbed as the aloe-covered finger gently but unfailingly targeted her emblem of purity. When the maidenhead was again confirmed, her mother's face relaxed and the sad chanting turned into a joyful noise. She withdrew her hand, opened her happy, glistening eyes, leaned forward, and kissed Michelette on the forehead. She rose, and at the door, turned. "Good night, my little flower," she whispered. "I love you."

Michelette rolled on her side, her back facing her mother. "Good night, Mama." She knew without looking that her mother waited at the door for the rest. Finally, she turned over and faced her mother. "I love you too, Mama." Her mother smiled and turned.

"Mama."

Her mother looked over her shoulder. "Yes?"

Tears blurred her mother's stooped image. Michelette started to say never mind, but couldn't. "Would you still love me if I failed the test?" Her mother just stared, then abruptly turned and yanked the door shut.

Michelette, knowing that she faced a miserable weekend, cried herself to sleep.

Pearl's Marriage

The next morning, Pearl went for a swim then met Wayne for breakfast under the almond trees across the pool from the dining terrace. After ordering toast and a plate of fresh papaya, mango, and pineapple, she asked, "Is there anything specific you'd like to do today?"

"I'd like to see if I could get in some tennis," Wayne replied. "Other than that, I planned just to spend the time with you. Anything you have in mind?"

"Well, I thought it'd be nice to spend the afternoon looking around the art galleries in Pétionville, then catching dinner at Lé St. Pierre's. An artist I know, Francois Mondesir, has some of her works at Gallery Nadar. You might be interested."

"In the works or the artist?"

"The works, but I'm sure you'd be interested in Francois if you ever met her. Come up to St. Jude, and I'll arrange it."

"Maybe next time. I have to be back at work Monday."

"Are you seeing anyone special?"

Wayne hesitated. "Nope."

"Nobody?"

"No, Mom. Nobody."

"You know, you're over thirty and not seeing anyone. Beverly is getting close to thirty and not seeing anyone. Why?"

"Well," Wayne said, "what's the point? Have a relationship like you and Dad? Who needs it?"

Pearl stared at Wayne. They had discussed this matter before, and she thought they had gone beyond it. Obviously she was wrong. "Our relationship wasn't bad until the last," she said.

"Come on, Mom. You and Dad didn't have a marriage. You had a business arrangement, and that's not what either Bev or I want. Yet that's what we're both scared we'll end up with. And, frankly, we'd both rather be single than have that."

Pearl used her fork and separated the fruit on her plate in three neat stacks. Maybe her marriage had been a business arrangement. But isn't that really what all marriages are? She and Ted maintained separate checking accounts and contributed monthly to the common account. Ted insisted from the start that they share everything fifty-fifty, but, since he made more than she and she shouldered more of the household duties, they ultimately negotiated the sixty-forty split. She knew of some couples who put everything into a joint checking account, but when she made that suggestion after they were married, Ted went ballistic. She never broached the subject again. Maybe that's where the notion that she had prostituted herself came from. But if it had been necessary to prostitute herself for the sake of her children, then fine. Besides, submitting to your husband was the law of the Church. It was a sin not to do so. Love, honor, and obey were in the marriage vows, and she always tried to follow Church law. She had done nothing wrong. Ted, of course, had. Many times he had committed adultery. She never had, even though she had opportunities. He demanded a divorce. She could not give it. In a fit of anger, he had hit her. She obeyed God's law and shouldn't have to defend her actions. Yet she felt confused. Something didn't seem right. Anyway, there was nothing she could do about it now.

"Mom. Are you okay?"

Pearl's attention snapped back. "Yes, I'm fine."

"How are you getting on at school?"

"Fine." She wanted to say that the past three years had been the happiest of her life, but didn't. How could a mother, a good mother, tell one of her children that the happiest years of her life had been when she was by herself? That was sad. It wasn't normal. Suddenly she felt like crying. Was this just a mood swing, one of those change of life things? Get out the fan. That'll hide it. She reached for her purse, dug out the folding fan, and began fanning herself.

"What's wrong, Mom?"

"Nothing." She took a sip of coffee. "Just something every woman my age has to go through. I'll be okay in a moment." She used the fan to shoo flies from her unfinished fruit.

"You sure?"

"Yes." She was lying. She wasn't sure. She didn't know what the hell was wrong. "I think I better go lie down in the air conditioning. Why don't we skip lunch and meet out front about one thirty?" She pushed her chair back and rose.

Wayne pushed his chair back. "I'll walk you to your room."

"No, please. I'll be fine."

Dinner with Wayne

Pearl waited under the front portico as Wayne approached.

"Feeling better?" he asked.

She wasn't going to tell him that she went back to her room and cried. "Much. I took a nap and just relaxed. Perhaps the week took its toll on me."

The man in a white Panama hat walked toward them. "Here comes that man I fell into yesterday. Now don't say a thing."

"Okay," Wayne said.

The man smiled warmly. "The clerk said that the shuttle was taking you folks into Pétionville. I'm going on through to Kenscoff. Mind if we share the van?"

"Not at all," Wayne replied.

"That'd be fine," Pearl answered.

"Good," the man said, extending his hand to Wayne. "I'm Bob Turner."

"Wayne Johnson, and this is my mother, Pearl."

Pearl held out her hand for Bob. His firm hand gently grasped hers. She saw the sudden look of recognition.

"Oh, yes. Yesterday. Front desk. How are you?"

He had such a soft, friendly manner. "I'm fine, just a little clumsy at times. I'd hoped you'd forgotten. That was so embarrassing."

"No need," Bob said as the shuttle pulled up. "Merely an accident." He opened the door, motioned for Pearl to take the seat beside the driver, and supported her elbow as she climbed in.

"Thank you," Pearl said.

"You're welcome." He and Wayne got into the van's second seat. As they drove off, Bob asked, "What brings you folks to Haiti?"

"I'm just down visiting her," Wayne said, nodding toward his mother.

"Oh," Bob said, looking at Pearl, "do you live here?"

Pearl shifted in the seat so she could see him. "I'm a lay teacher at a Catholic school near here." She comfortably went on to tell about St. Jude but did not get a chance to finish before the van pulled to a stop at the open market in Pétionville. "Wow!" she exclaimed, looking around. "That was quick. This is our stop." She opened the door. Then she surprised herself. "Perhaps we can continue the conversation this evening?" She and Wayne got out, and Bob changed to the front seat. Through the open window, he said, "I'd like that, providing I get back. I'm visiting a friend and might be late, but I would like to hear more about the school."

As the van drove away, Wayne said, "Nice fellow, isn't he?"

"I suppose."

Wayne smiled.

"What?"

"Nothing."

They strolled over to and up Rue Clarveaux, dodging local shoppers and passing many street vendors hawking shoes, T-shirts, dresses, sport coats, suits, and all types of Haitian folk art.

Pétionville, metropolitan Port-au-Prince's exclusive suburb, sits on the Port-au-Prince side of the mountain range that splits the southern provinces of Haiti. Due to its high elevation, the climate was usually dry and relatively cool. Pearl carried her jacket, knowing that she would need it after the sun went down.

As they walked along, they dodged plastic bottles strewn along the sidewalk, avoided holes in the concrete, and sidestepped trash piles. If you want something, you can find it in Pétionville, but it could be rather expensive and somewhat difficult if you don't know your way around. Pearl stopped at the window of an exclusive dress shop. She admired a black and white fashion that the sign said was straight from Paris.

She turned to Wayne. "Mind if I go inside for a minute?"

"Nope," he said, leaning against the corner post. "I'll wait here."

Pearl entered the boutique. Immediately a slender, deeply tanned thirty-something woman wearing a lovely brown and white silk dress with a tan belt approached. "May I assist you?" she asked.

"Actually, I'm just looking, thank you."

"Look all you want," the attendant replied.

Pearl glanced at the dresses, none of which had a price tag. She took one from the rack, a black number with large white buttons and matching collar, turned toward the mirror, and held it in front of her. "Not bad," she mumbled.

"You would look stunning in that," the attendant said.

"It is nice. How much is it?"

"Only three hundred sixty-five American."

"That's a bit more than I can pay right now," Pearl replied, still facing the mirror imagining herself in it. "I'll just have to dream about it tonight." She handed the dress to the woman and walked out.

Wayne stood next to the shop watching two mechanics change the front tire on a large dump truck, its front end raised by a block and tackle suspended from the limb of a royal poinciana. A used tire fence lined the back of the lot.

"Zoning laws aren't enforced here, are they?" Wayne asked.

"To my knowledge, zoning laws don't exist," Pearl replied, stepping over a black stream of oil leading to the street. "Right up here is Expressions Galleria. Let's browse through there. You may find something you like. After that, we'll go over to get some espresso at Galata."

Pearl enjoyed the overall atmosphere of Pétionville's art district on Saturdays. It was exciting to dodge the shoppers and hawkers, step around the paid car watchers, and avoid the traffic on its way to and from wherever. Pétionville was always on the move. People were everywhere. Cars and pedestrians alike negotiated their way, some waving cars on, drivers waving pedestrians across, but everyone always moving. Wayne said its busyness reminded him of an anthill that God had just stepped on.

After espresso, Pearl guided Wayne to Gallery Nadar, the gallery that had exclusive rights to Francois's works. It was the first time Wayne had seen art by a Haitian master, and he was astounded. After examining each of Francois's pieces, he said, "This one would look great over the couch in my office."

"Better ask the price before you get carried away," his mother advised.

Wayne looked at the number on the painting, then went to the gallery attendant, a beautiful maple-skinned lady about twenty-five dressed in what appeared to be a fashion from the store Pearl had visited. "Could you look up the price on M-forty-three?"

"That's a Francois Mondesir," the attendant replied, turning the pages of her price book and running her inch-long magenta fingernail down the sheet. "Sixty-five hundred dollars U.S."

"Whoa," Wayne exclaimed. "That's a little more than I intended."

"That's what most people say." She smiled graciously. "Let me show you something that may be a little more in your price range. Can you give me some idea where it will be displayed?"

"I've in mind something to go over a couch in my office. I'll be looking at it almost every day."

"Well, a Mondesir is definitely overpriced for decorator art. Her work is already at the collector and museum level. However, the works of some of our lesser-known artists who are almost as talented may be suitable and a very good buy. Let me show you several."

Pearl marveled at the attendant's skill. She had Wayne hooked. Of course, it didn't hurt to have a model's body complemented by the face of an angel.

Her svelte hips made Pearl promise herself not to indulge in a chocolate eclair at Pierre's.

Pearl and Wayne chatted with the beauty while the three-hundred-fifty-dollar modern oil by some artist about whom he could care less was packaged for carrying on the plane. After they left the gallery, Pearl asked, "Did you get her name?"

"Yes," Wayne answered, the package tucked under his arm, "but she's married and has two children."

Pearl, visualizing the attendant's trim body, winced inside, then salved her conscience by telling herself that age would catch up. "Did you find that out before or after you bought the painting?"

"After," Wayne said, dejected. "Now don't say it, Mom."

"Say what? We women know that all men think with the same thing. I knew she had you the moment she fluttered those fake eyelashes."

"You had to get that in somewhere, didn't you?" Wayne said as he stopped her from stepping in front of a car. "She was beautiful, wasn't she?"

"As are many Haitian women."

They dodged pedestrians, hawkers, and a sidewalk food cart before stopping in front of the Café dé Arts. "I tried to get us in here tonight to hear this show," she said, pointing to a poster advertising the instrumental group Strings and singer James Germain, "but it was sold out."

"Never heard of 'em."

"Strings is Haiti's premier instrumental group, and James Germain has perhaps the Caribbean's most golden voice. They seldom play together, but when they do, it is an evening to behold. Their rendition of 'Merci Bon Dieu' will have you crying your eyes out."

"Really?"

"Yes. 'Merci Bon Dieu' is, for lack of a better description, a ballad describing the Haitian condition and predicting that someday the poverty will end. Believe me, it'll tug at your heart to experience the majesty of their music." She paused and walked away. "But maybe some other time. Anyway, let's get on over to Pierre's."

After another stint of playing dodge the people, cars, and numerous pieces of discarded plastic, and wincing at the occasional whiff of rotting trash, they walked under the lavender bougainvillea-covered arch into Pierre's. The maitre d' stored Wayne's package then led them to a secluded table near a small artificial waterfall, snapping his fingers to a waiter along the way. They sat, and a waiter, wearing a white waistcoat and royal blue trousers, brought them a complimentary pony of Grand Marnier and explained the evening's dishes; lemon baked salmon, almond chicken, rack of lamb with fresh mint, and grilled vegetables with minced mango chutney on a bed of saffron rice. Each meal, of course, custom prepared. Pearl chose the salmon, and Wayne selected the rack of lamb and a bottle of French white zinfandel, a compromise between white for Pearl and red to complement his lamb.

As the waiter left, Wayne asked, "Mom, why don't you write Bev and explain your viewpoints?"

"I've tried many times to do just that, but each time it sounds like I'm defending my position rather than explaining it. I don't think I can."

The waiter returned and set down a basket with a loaf of fresh, warm sliced French bread wrapped in white linen, kept warm by a miniature hot water bottle. Beside it he placed a small bowl filled with chilled pieces of fleur-de-lis shaped butter. The wine steward quickly followed with an ice bucket and bottle of wine. In proper wine fashion, he allowed Wayne to examine the bottle, then removed the cork and passed it for him. Wayne sniffed and nodded. The steward poured a dram in Wayne's stem. He swirled it, examined the wine's legs, sniffed its bouquet, took a sip, and expressed approval. The steward served Pearl, then filled Wayne's glass.

"You don't have to be defensive, Mom," he said, buttering a slice of bread. "You must have had good reasons. When you first got married, surely you and Dad loved each other. Start there. Explain your love, then try to explain where it went sour. I know Bev would appreciate the attempt, even if she might not agree."

"Wayne, you just don't know how often I've thought of doing that. I tried even before Ted and I split, but I don't want to say any bad things about Ted. He was a good provider. He kept up his end of the marriage." She tasted her wine.

"Like having all those girlfriends was keeping his end of the marriage? I don't buy that at all, Mom."

"You knew?"

"Mom, come on! You can't be serious."

"I didn't think you knew. Did he tell you?"

"Mom, we've known since elementary school. Everybody knew, except maybe you. Hell, we used to draw pictures of his girlfriends and stick them with pins."

Pearl shrugged her shoulders. "Oh, I knew, all right." She ran her finger around the edge of the wine stem. "I just looked the other way." She took a longer sip.

"Why?"

Pearl squinted at Wayne, trying to look into his soul. For the first time, she saw him not only as her son, but as the adult he was. She was tired of holding it all inside.

"What the hell. We're adults. I might as well say it." She drained her glass of wine and signaled the steward, who rushed over and refilled it. "I was a coward. I knew every time he had a girlfriend. I didn't know who. Didn't care. You'll find out that there are times when you just don't interfere when you're scared of the things you might hear or have to do."

"Why didn't you end it when you first found out?"

She looked at him, then sipped more courage. "Ted was handsome, big man on campus, and president of his fraternity. My father tried to warn me about him, but I wouldn't listen. Then I got pregnant with you, and we had to get married." She stared at him. "Surprised?"

"Geez, Mom. We can count. We've known that all along. In labor two days to deliver a nine-pound-six-ounce premature baby boy! Get real."

71

Pearl drank more, and it felt good. "I feel better just having said it. Anyway, the first time he played around was about six months after we got married, just before you came. I found out later that he was with a girl when you were born." She took another tiny swallow. "When you're young, you think you can change people. I thought I could change him. Besides, I was going to make my marriage work. Well, if you never remember anything I tell you, remember this— you don't marry a person to change them, you marry to live with them." She took another swallow. "Am I embarrassing you?"

"Not at all." Wayne buttered a slice of warm bread.

"Want to hear more?" Pearl said, following suit.

"Sure." He took a bite.

"Well, I thought I could compete with the bimbos, so I tried. Lord, how I tried." She took another swallow. "Of course, I thought everything was okay. I carefully practiced Vatican roulette. Naturally, that led to Beverly. From there everything went downhill. I found out that he even tried to make out with Rose."

"Aunt Rose?"

"Yes, Aunt Rose. Can you believe? You remember she was always over at the house after school watching you two til I got there, then she'd go home. Remember that just after daddy died, she moved in with us? She was only sixteen. About four months later, she went to live at a girlfriend's house. You remember all that?"

"Uh-huh."

"Well, after Ted and I split, Rose told me that the night before she left, when I was at a PTA meeting, he came into her room, exposed himself, and tried to get her to go to bed with him. She left and spent that night with a friend and moved out the next day. Without an explanation. Dumb, blind me!" She drained her last drops and signaled the steward, who refilled her glass. A tad of wine remained in the bottle, so he placed it back in the bucket.

"You still haven't said why you didn't leave earlier." He ate another slice of the bread.

"The marriage vow said for better or worse till death do us part. I couldn't leave. I made my oath before God. So I did the best I could. I really tried." She sipped more wine. "God, did I try. Mama used to tell me that the efforts behind a successful marriage were 95 percent the woman's and 5 percent the man's. How right she was. And at school! The sisters pounded into us that divorce is a sin. If my marriage failed, then I was a failure. Doomed to hell." She took another swallow. "I couldn't. Do you understand that?"

"Yep, and that's what you should tell Bev."

"I did, or at least part. She said that I was dumb not to sue for divorce." Tears welled up. "Shit. Now I'm getting melancholy." She wiped her eyes. "Bev said I had no self-respect and should break free from those stupid rules."

"What did you say?"

"I told her that a woman's self-respect is secondary to her husband, marriage, and children." Pearl looked around. "Damn, the service is slow. Where the hell is our food?"

Wayne put his hand on her arm. "Mother, perhaps you better calm down a bit."

"'Mother? I must be getting drunk." She tasted her bread. "You know what Bev said when I told her that?"

"I can imagine." He was grinning.

"Bullshit!"

"'Bullshit?, I can't imagine?" Wayne asked.

"No! That's what she said. 'Bullshit!'"

Wayne chuckled. "She always did cut to the chase."

Pearl laughed and looked around. The alcohol had lifted her thick veil of societal propriety. "Is our food ever coming? Only the French have a way to make people believe that lousy service is really fine dining. Let's get another bottle of wine." She reached over, snatched the bottle from the ice bucket, emptied it into her glass, and waved it in the air until the wine steward acknowledged. Wayne, splitting with silent laughter, buried his face in his hands.

"Now I'm embarrassing you, aren't I?"

"Actually, I'm enjoying seeing you unwind and relax. I don't think I've ever seen you let your hair down like this."

"Is something wrong with my hair?" She grabbed her purse.

"No, Mom." He chuckled. "It's just an expression. You look fine." He glanced over her shoulder. "Here come our dinners."

She turned and looked. "Well, it's about goddamn time!"

Wayne laughed, then looked around, obviously chagrined. "Mom, please kinda hold it down."

"Your face is red."

"No kidding." They both snickered and refrained from bursting out in hysterics as the waiter elegantly served the dinners. The wine steward approached. Wayne shook his head. The steward nodded and retreated.

"Think I've had enough?"

"I think maybe you better slow down."

They enjoyed the meal and each finished with a chocolate eclair and espresso. Afterward, Wayne, through the maitre d', arranged for a taxi to take them back to the Creole.

Pearl, happy and giddy, strolled into the hotel. "See, I can still walk straight." From the corridor she glanced over the bar and spotted an empty cocktail table. "Come on, let's have a nightcap."

"Mother," Wayne said, his painting tucked under his arm.

"Don't mother me. My room's right over there." She pointed toward the annex. "Come on." She took him by the arm and led him down the steps to the table. He leaned his painting against the edge as Pearl pulled out a chair and sat. Then she looked up and spotted Bob Turner walking through the portico. "Oh, oh." She sprang from her chair.

"What?" Wayne asked.

With her head, she beckoned toward Bob. "I'm not going to let him see me like this." She quickly ducked around the edge of the bar and made a straight line to her room, Wayne following close behind. At her door, she fumbled in her purse for the room key then remembered that she had left it at the front desk. "Wayne, hon, would you?"

"Sure." He walked away, but, over his shoulder, said, "But I forgot and left my painting by the table so I'll ask Mr. Turner to bring it."

"Don't you dare!" she exclaimed as he turned the corner. She was sure that he was only kidding, but not leaving anything to chance, hid in the shadows beneath an overhanging bougainvillea until he approached— alone. He handed the key to her, put his arm around her shoulder, and pecked her on the cheek. "Good night, Mom. I love you."

"I love you, too." She unlocked the door, and Wayne walked away.

"Wayne," she called.

He stopped and turned.

"I really enjoyed tonight."

"So did I."

Pearl closed the door to her room, stripped, and climbed into the tub for another long, soaking bath. As she lounged in warm water, her brain spun like a figure skater. Thoughts whirled through her mind. Wayne. Love. Beverly. Love. Ted. What? St. Jude's. Love. Francois. Michelette. Love. Hate. Beverly. Letter. Must keep trying. Write letter tomorrow. She loved her children. Didn't Moland say that love was a very complicated subject? What did he mean by that? What's complicated about love? Either you do or you don't.

The Rules

She Dances

Pearl, wearing a one piece purple and white bathing suit and lavender terry cloth cover-up, sat beneath the almond tree canopy, doodling on a piece of paper, flipping her thongs off and on, nursing a better-than-average, uncommon hangover. She laid the pencil on the breakfast table and lifted the third cup of strong black coffee to her lips, hoping to dampen her mouth's cotton lining. Dry toast was all she could handle from the lavish brunch bar. Wayne, who had left for the airport at nine, assured her that she did nothing to embarrass herself and suggested that she not accompany him on the thirty-minute trip down the winding, bumpy road to the airport. She was grateful.

While cradling the cup in her hands, she silently swished the strong brew around in her mouth. Gently placing the cup back on its saucer, she stared at the paper. Several times she had started a letter to Beverly, several times scratched through her sentences, tucked the sheet under the stack, and begun again.

"Would you like more coffee?" the waiter asked, startling Pearl from her thoughts.

"A warm-up would be fine, thank you."

"We have some fresh pineapple juice. May I bring you a glass?"

"No, but a glass of ice water would be refreshing." The waiter walked away, and she took her wristwatch from the pocket of her cover-up. For more than an hour, she had been sitting there trying to write something. She shooed a fly off the toast.

"Good morning," came a male voice. Pearl looked down toward the pool's rim and saw Bob Turner, both arms resting on the pool skirt, looking at her. An auburn tint reflected from the thick band of wet hair surrounding his almost bald top. His hairy arms had the same auburn hue. She scarcely recognized him without his white Panama.

"Good morning," Pearl replied.

"Did you enjoy last evening?"

She smiled. "Perhaps too much. How was Kenscoff?"

"Fine. My friend up there runs the school and helps at the Baptist Mission hospital."

The waiter set a goblet of ice water on the table. "Thank you," Pearl said, then returned her attention to Bob. "I've been there. Their school and ours are part of a network of private schools here in Haiti." She took a swallow of water.

"What type of network?"

"Mainly to swap supplies. Often schools in Haiti get donations we can't use, but others can. Some years ago the schools got together and formed a network where we can swap things back and forth. Sometimes we temporarily swap teachers as well. Did you happen to go into their bookstore?"

Gray streaks peppered his sideburns.

"Yes. I bought a book called *Survival Creole*. I figure since I'm going to be down here off and on during the next several years, I should learn enough of the language to get along. Sorry I didn't get back so you could tell me about your school. What's the name of it again?"

"St. Jude's. Up near St. Marc. It's a small Catholic mission school. I think you'll find Creole interesting and, if you have any aptitude for languages, relatively easy. I've learned to speak it fairly well."

"Would you be interested in tutoring the next time I come down? I'll pay the going rate."

Her insides jumped. Her hand shook. "I've never tutored an adult in Creole, but if it could be worked out, I'd consider it."

Bob started to back away from the edge. "Good. Are you going to be around this afternoon? Perhaps we could talk more?"

"Yes," she replied. "I'd like that. Please give me a call." She gave him her room number.

Bob repeated the number then said, "Sorry to interrupt your writing." He kicked off the side of the pool and backstroked away.

He had broad shoulders and a strong chest.

Pearl watched out of the corner of her eye as he swam six laps then easily hoisted himself from the pool and dried off. The small roll above his swimsuit suggested that at one time he was overweight but had lost most of it. He slipped into a maroon shirt, wrapped the towel around his neck, and, just as he entered the garden, glanced her way. A warm glow swept over her, and it wasn't the beginning of the normal hot flash. This one, to her, was new. And exciting. Yet natural.

She stared at the blank sheet and tapped the table with the eraser end of the pencil while trying to regain her concentration and start again to write Beverly. Absentmindedly, she fidgeted with her hair, twisting strands with her fingers the way seasoned spaghetti-eaters wind pasta on a fork. Inadvertently, she wound her hair too tight and pulled it. She untangled her fingers and smiled, recalling an incident at school when she was only nine. The class project was a puppet show. While the class made backdrops, glue became the weapon of choice, ultimately covering most students' hands and portions of clothing. As the sister firmly brought order and reminded the class of the proper procedures for handling sticky substances, Pearl's hand got stuck in her hair. The nun had to cut it away, and Pearl had a lopsided haircut for more than four months. Another time, while finger painting, she came home with orange and green streaks in her hair. The girls at school thought it cool, but what her mother couldn't scrub out, she cut out. Funny, she thought, the things we carry imbedded in our subconscious.

Maybe that was how she should approach the letter to Beverly. What imbedded notions of love and respect between mother and daughter had Pearl inherited and inadvertently passed on to her daughter? Would that help Bev understand? Pearl thought she'd had a typical childhood. She had been born in Tampa, Florida, the fourth of five children. Her parents, both Irish immigrants, were Catholics. All the children, reared

under conservative Catholic doctrine, were sent to a
private Irish Catholic mission school.

Her father worked hard, domineered the family,
and was a strict disciplinarian. If any of the children
disobeyed, he wielded the razor strap he brought from
Ireland. A heavy drinker, he often came home drunk,
and the children were careful not to make any noise.
Most often they left and went to a friend's house. She
recalled being awakened many nights by him and her
mother yelling and calling each other names. Several
times he had hit her mother. Always, after he sobered
up, they professed sorrow and made up. And her
mother went to confession, usually confessing that the
fight had been her fault and asking forgiveness. She
used to tell the girls that life was not intended to be
easy, that people, particularly women, were put on
earth to suffer just as Jesus suffered, and He said the
meek shall inherit the earth. From this, Pearl recalled
thinking that suffering and meekness were admirable
traits, particularly for women.

She lifted the goblet and took another sip of water
as her mind flitted to her father and mother. He had
been a good provider, which, according to him, was his
role in God's grand scheme. They had a comfortable
home in an average neighborhood near Hyde Park, a
suburb of Tampa, and were reasonably well clothed,
fed, and educated; words that Pearl absentmindedly
jotted down. Her mother had died of a massive
cerebral hemorrhage not long after Pearl's wedding.
Her father died twelve years later of lung cancer. At
the time of his death, Rose, being the youngest by
twenty years, was the only child left at home. He had

left sufficient insurance for her to become a registered nurse.

Pearl doodled while she studied the list. Then she wrote the word "love" and put a big question mark beside it. Where was love in the formula? Moland had referred to love. What exactly was love? A sudden chill rushed through her body as though the word scared her.

She jotted down childhood fears and listed spiders and roaches. Those were both normal. Then she listed death. Why, she asked herself, had death come to mind? She recalled the sisters at school. They said that when people died and went to heaven, they spent eternity with our Father, God. She remembered as a little girl being terrified of her father. She thought that she loved her father, though she couldn't ever remember telling him that or, for that matter, him saying that he loved her. And she certainly didn't like it when, for no reason, he brought out the razor strap. She thought of one rainy day in particular. The kids had been playing in the house and got a bit rowdy. Without warning, her father got the strap, lined them all up, made them pull their pants down, and struck each twice on their bare rumps. She recalled thinking that if God was like her father, she wasn't all that anxious to spend eternity with him.

She remembered another time in Bible class, they were being taught about sinners and baptisms, and she asked why little babies who couldn't even talk were considered sinners until they were baptized. Well, the sister reacted as though she was in the presence of Satan himself. She said that all people are born sinners and stayed that way until baptized and sanctified, and that the sisters were God's messengers, sent there to help people along the way to sanctification, including children who asked insolent questions. Pearl recalled thinking that if the sisters were messengers from God, then what must God be like?

Another time at school a sister dragged Pearl to the principal's office where she got whipped with a yardstick, then had to turn and thank the principal for helping her see the error of her ways. She was told that God was angry and impatient with those who didn't obey his laws. Neither her father nor the sisters at the school did anything to assuage this concept. In those early years, she learned that everything would be fine if, without question, she obeyed the rules.

As she got older, her mother and school taught her that the primary reason God created women was to have babies, and that women who participated in sex without intent of multiplying were committing mortal sin. Not only that, but because Eve caused Adam's fall from grace, it was emphasized during her formative years that some inherently evil desire worked through women, a force they had to continually repress.

One of the problems she and Ted always had was with sex. He pressured her to use a diaphragm, which was a sin. She did get fitted for one but chose, unknown to Ted, to practice the rhythm method, a Church-approved form of birth control. She recalled thinking that her Beverly pregnancy was a form of punishment for attempting to interfere with God's will.

Then she recollected the Wednesday afternoon her mother was called to school. Her oldest sister, Patsy, who was in the eleventh grade at the time, had, according to the principal, been grossly irreverent to one of the nuns. According to student legend, Patsy asked if the intent of using the rhythm method was for birth control, what was the real difference between using such a low percentage method or using a higher percentage form like a condom or diaphragm? Patsy was verbally reprimanded in front of the entire class, then ushered quickly to the principal's office for punishment. She had to stay home for the remainder of the week and do penance ten times every day under her mother's direct supervision, or be expelled from school.

Pearl was an adult now and knew that many of those childhood notions were just that, but how could she summarize to Beverly without seeming to make excuses or being defensive? Perhaps her greatest failing was not thinking about the spirit behind the practices. It was much easier to follow the rules without question on the premise that they were for the good of all.

Pearl laid the pencil down and took another drink of water. She stood, pulled off her cover, and stepped into the pool. She'd worry about the letter another time.

She swam for a half-hour, dried off, and went to her room. A message hung on the door handle. It said that the Hotel El Rancho had a special dance band and complimentary hors d'oeuvres that evening and, as a courtesy to the patrons of la Villa Creole, all cover charges would be waived, and drinks for ladies would be half price. It would be necessary to stop at the front desk for a pass. She opened her door thinking that the last thing she wanted was a drink, much less several. Still, El Rancho was only a block away. She rinsed her hair and stretched out across the bed.

The phone jarred her from a deep sleep. "Hello."

"This is Bob Turner. Sounds like I woke you. I'm sorry."

"No problem," she said, glancing at her watch. "Wow, four-thirty. I really didn't intend to sleep at all, much less this long."

"Then you must have needed it. Care to join me by the pool?"

Company with a contemporary adult American male would be a nice change of pace, she thought. "Sure. Fifteen or twenty minutes okay?"

"Fine. See you then."

Pearl hung up. She didn't know what she would wear. The blue and gold outfit was too dressy, yet the lavender and white sun dress that she planned on wearing back to St. Jude's the next day might be considered too casual. She thought for a minute, then dug into the overnight case and pulled out a white shawl she used occasionally as a shoulder wrap during the chilly prelude to a hot flash. She draped it over her shoulders, stood in front of the mirror and turned first to one side then the other. It didn't look too old. She slipped into the lavender, brushed her hair, quickly powdered her face, and again checked herself in the mirror to make sure the scar didn't show and that the shawl and dress didn't clash. She put the room key in her purse, and walked out to meet Bob Turner.

She was nervous. And scared. Was this the equivalent of a date? Was she, a married woman, flirting with sin?

Francois and Georges

In her studio, palette in hand, Francois impatiently made quick, darting jabs, trying to obtain just the right bold red color. She couldn't concentrate. Since noon she had felt Georges's presence. Eagerly, she listened for the gong. It had been more than two weeks since he had sailed with his two fishing boats to catch the migrating fish. Normally the boats would come back in for the weekend, but this time they had not. That was why Georges was so successful. When it was time to work, he worked, and when it was time to play, he played. He was like her, not one to be tied to a schedule. He followed his own nature.

Georges Jean Charles was two years older than she. They had met nine years earlier when he beached his rowboat on St. Jude's property to see if the school wanted to buy some fish. She had been in the Shelter, reviewing student art. He wandered in and watched. He chatted with Moland and enjoyed some of Natti's cookies. At first, he sold small quantities but soon, he was there almost every Thursday donating substantial amounts of seafood. Occasionally he joined the staff for dinner. After several months, Moland invited Georges to participate in one of the discussion sessions.

As time passed, they found out that Georges belonged to the sea. When only a fourth-level student at a local school, he carved a small dugout, which was now a beautiful planter enshrined just inside Francois's gate, from a log that drifted up on shore. One day when he was out in the shallows he netted several Caribbean lobsters. One he recognized as a female because of the orange bundle of eggs on its underbelly. Instinctively, he reasoned that if he took the female, there would be less lobster next time. He placed her back and watched her streak to safety. The same day, as he beached his dugout, a white man saw the lobsters and offered to buy them. Georges's commercial fishing business was born.

He had a passion for the sea. Local fisherman said that he was blessed with the senses of a fish and claimed he could understand the sounds of the ocean. And his reputation for dependability cornered the lucrative resort market along the southwestern shore of Point St. Marc. Passionately dedicated to his profession, he quickly became the local fishery expert and had begun an aquaculture farm, raising freshwater tilapia to supply the hotels of Port-au-Prince and Jacmel.

Almost from the beginning Francois and Georges knew they were meant for each other. They had discussed marriage but concluded that the institution, in the accepted sense, suited neither. As Moland counseled during one of their many talk sessions, their relationship was born of God. They would be together forever, but, for them to reach their full capacity for love, they had to let the winds of life dance between them, otherwise both would suffocate. During another session, Francois emphatically stated that she would rather be Georges's whore than to restrict him from being the best he could be, and he professed that he would rather be considered a kept man and have no descendants than to detract her from being the artist she had to be. Even Father Mike said that they could not be tied to each other otherwise the rope of love, being so tightly wound, would ultimately strangle both. They maintained separate lives, yet when not involved with their individual passions, were always together.

She knew Georges was near. She could feel him. She paused from her halfhearted attempt at painting and strained to hear the sound of his truck. Nothing. Yet the song of the wind told her that he was close. Then it came. Three short blasts of a boat's horn rattled the windows. She looked out to the gulf. Much to her delight, she saw a familiar trawler, its drying nets drooping from the booms, slowing. "Georges!" she exclaimed to the wind as the horn again blasted. She tossed aside her palette and brush and ran waving to the beach.

One of the three barely discernable men on deck waved back, tossed two bundles over the side, and dove in. When Georges surfaced, he grabbed the floating packages and tied them around himself. A crewman handed the swimmer something resembling a long stemmed flower, which he gripped with his teeth and swam toward shore, the bundles trailing behind. Francois, fully clothed, ran into the water and waded toward the swimmer as fast as she could. They met in breast-deep water where Georges, his sienna, muscular body towering six inches over her, took the perfectly formed white calla lily from his mouth. "A beauty for a beauty, with love." Tears of happiness welled up as she took the flower and looked into his ebony eyes. "I've missed you," he said.

She wrapped her arms around his neck and legs around his waist. "Me, too." They kissed. The fishing boat gave three short blasts. Both of them, cheek to cheek, looked seaward and waved as the vessel chugged off. Georges easily hoisted Francois and carried her toward shore, the bundles still trailing. "The lily's gorgeous," she said, cradling the flower. "Where'd you find it?"

"I picked it on the Isle of Gonave two days ago. Kept it in cold storage until now."

"Well, I love it."

"I knew you'd appreciate its almost perfect natural beauty. And it reminded me so much of you." He kissed her and whispered, "I do love you."

She hugged him tightly. Tears streamed from her eyes. "I love you, too."

Just before they reached shore, he put her down and lifted his trailing packages, a waterproof bag and a net sack containing two squirming lobsters. "And I've got to do something with these. What do you say we have a picnic this evening here on the beach?" He unhooked the lobster sack and weighted it in the edge of the water with a large stone.

"Well, I'd say something like I'd be delighted." She studied the flower. "I've got to get this into a vase."

"And I've got to shower."

"I'll join you as soon as I can." She rushed into the studio as he walked into the house.

89

Georges was already in the shower lathering the washcloth when Francois, who had left her clothes scattered between the studio and house, joined him. "Here, let me," she said, taking the cloth and soap from him. "You don't know how long these last two weeks have been." She scrubbed concentric circles on his chest, stood on her tiptoes and brushed his lips with hers. Warm water from the solar storage tank drizzled from the showerhead and carved brown valleys in the soapy lather on Georges's solid body. She touched her body to his. "I've really missed you." She lathered each cheek and again brushed his lips.

"I've missed you, too. It's been a very long two weeks."

She pressed her hips against him and wriggled. "It doesn't show."

A broad smile crossed Georges's face. "Yet."

She rubbed the heavily soaped cloth over his already foamy broad shoulders, down his massive chest, and across his rippled abdomen to his firm waist. "You keep in such good shape. One of these days, when you're going to be around long enough, I'd like to try a plaster sculpture."

"Okay, but not this time. I've got to pick up some fingerlings at Croix Des Bouquets Wednesday and get them up to Pont Sonde," he said as she moved around his body and scrubbed his back. "Oh, that feels good." He flexed his shoulder muscles.

"I'm just happy we have a couple of days." She finished lathering his firm posterior, then knelt and scrubbed the tops of both feet. "Tonight should be fun. The moon is almost full."

"You bring enough light without the moon."

His company pleased her. She happily washed her way up past his knees. As she lathered his thighs, he turned, and she tenderly washed his excitement.

"Careful. It's been awhile."

She rose, gently kissed him, and handed him the cloth. "Your turn."

Francois closed her eyes. Georges, using a touch softer than a powder puff, dabbed her cheeks with the warm cloth. Then he kissed her, first on closed eyelids, then the nose, lips, and chin. He caressingly washed her breasts then titillated each with a single flick of his tongue while washing her stomach. He knelt and cleansed her legs and feet as warm mist filled the shower. He turned her around. The warm glow of expectation grew brighter as he washed her limbs. His delicate touch as the washcloth guided up her thighs aroused eager anticipation. He stood, cupped each breast, and pulled her close, pressing his warm organ tightly against her. While caressing each shoulder, he kissed her neck. The washcloth slid down her body and dropped to the floor. He symbolically probed her ear with his tongue, then whispered again, "I love you." Her heart raced as enthusiastic sensations engulfed her. A delicate musk aroma filled the torrid shower.

With a musician's touch, he massaged the moist cluster of protective hair with a rhythmic circular motion while holding her close. He kissed her ear again then turned her sideways, tipped her head and licked, then kissed, her lips. Waves of euphoric expectation rubberized her legs. She twirled, gazed into his eyes, and, as her hungry lips touched his, circled her arms tightly around his glistening neck.

A blanket of emotional warmth engulfed her as warm water baptized their spirit as they simultaneously reaffirmed their eternal unity.

The Dance

Pearl stopped between the arches and surveyed the dining room and lounge area. She spotted Bob, an empty chair next to him, seated with several others around an oval dining table. Relieved yet somewhat disappointed that he wasn't alone, she made her way down the stairs. As she approached the table, Bob stood. The two other men at the table followed suit. A young slender lady sat between the two strangers.

Bob pulled out the chair for her. "This is Pearl Johnson," he said. "I apologize but I'm not sure I could pronounce each of your names, so please introduce yourself."

One gentleman younger than Bob grinned. "In other words, he forgot our names."

Bob laughed. "Pretty obvious, huh?"

The man winked. "When your name's Mac, it is. Most people can pronounce that. I'm Mac. Pleased to meet you, Pearl." He took Pearl's extended hand, then sat.

"And I'm Jacques," the other man said with a French accent as he placed his hand on the slim lady's shoulder, "and this is my friend, Cherie." He kissed Pearl's hand. "Pleased to meet you, madam."

"I'm happy to meet all of you."

"Would you like something to drink?" Bob asked.

Pearl remembered the previous night. "A glass of fruit punch, please."

Bob motioned for the waiter as he told Pearl that each had registered at the desk to go to El Rancho, and the desk clerk suggested they go together as a group. The waiter arrived, and Bob ordered Pearl's drink, and asked that it be put on his bill. As they finished their beverages and snacked on the fresh roasted peanuts, each told a little about themselves. Mac, married with two preteens, was a bureaucrat down auditing the local U.S.A.I.D. station. Jacques was a surgeon from France assisting at the General Hospital with surgical training. Cherie, so he said, was his surgical assistant.

Pearl's insides twitched when Bob told the group that he was widowed after a long marriage, and had three children, all grown and on their own. That news made her feel better about the evening, though she was somewhat confused about her own emotions. She felt queasy. Perhaps she was still nursing the remnants of last night.

Pearl told them about herself, that she and her husband had split, and that she had two grown children, also on their own. She deliberately kept to herself the fact that she was not divorced. She didn't lie. She just didn't tell the whole story. Yet her insides churned because she felt she had misled Bob into thinking she wasn't married. It really didn't matter, she rationalized, but she was uncomfortable and wasn't sure why.

The group walked over to El Rancho, stopping along the way to scan the Haitian art displayed on the fence along the road. They walked up the esplanade to the Georgian structure, entered the elegant foyer, and followed the big-band music wafting from the poolside dance floor where several couples swayed to a slow, sad rendition of "The Unchained Melody." The group found a large table beside the floor, and, before anyone could say anything, Jacques ordered two bottles of champagne. Pearl promised herself that she would not repeat the evening before. Bob held Pearl's chair, then sat next to her.

"They're butchering that song," Bob said. "It should be at least two beats faster."

"Oh," Pearl said as the music concluded, "you know music?"

"A little," Bob replied as the band concluded and two trumpeters joined the musicians and struck up "Pennies from Heaven."

"That sounds better. Would you care to dance?"

"Oh," Pearl said, somewhat taken aback. "I haven't danced in years."

He rose and took her by the hand. "But you have danced? Let's go."

"Yes," she said, unconsciously rising. "But it's been so long."

"It's like swimming. Once you do it, you never forget. Just follow my lead."

Pearl, self-conscious, followed Bob into the middle of the dance floor. She was thankful that several other couples joined them. Maybe nobody would notice how clumsy she was.

Bob's left hand found her right, and he, almost without her knowing it, guided her into the dance position. His right hand on her left shoulder blade felt reassuring.

"Relax. It'll come back."

What he didn't know was that the last time she had danced was at Ted's brother's wedding more than twenty years before.

"An easy fox trot," he said, gently pulling her as he backed into the dance.

Bob was obviously a good dancer. She felt awkward even though his guidance was gentle and consistent. She started counting to herself. *One and two. One and two. One and two.* Then they twirled and stepped in another direction. She stumbled but he, as he had at the front desk the first day they met, steadied her. She felt her face flush and was positive that everyone in the ballroom had seen her misstep.

"Relax," Bob said. "That was hardly noticeable."

His smile would melt her pre-flash chill.

"So say you." Pearl glanced around. "Everyone saw that." She stumbled again.

Bob laughed. "I know that's the way it feels, but my guess is that most of the people sitting around are wishing they knew how to dance, and are probably admiring how graceful you are."

"If so, they've got me fooled. I'm a nervous wreck."

"You're really an easy partner," Bob said, again smoothly switching direction. This time she did not trip.

"You'd make anyone look good."

"Thank you." He blushed. "I enjoy dancing. My wife was a dance instructor, so naturally we danced quite a bit."

"Competition?"

"A little, but we didn't find that very much fun."

The music stopped, then the band broke into "Ain't She Sweet."

"That's a gentle swing," Bob said. "Care to try it?"

"Perhaps the next one. Right now I have to calm my nerves."

They went back to the table and found Cherie sitting alone sipping champagne. Bob looked at Pearl. "Mind if I ask her?"

"Why, no," Pearl replied, thinking that it was considerate of him to ask her approval.

Cherie happily accepted, and Pearl watched the accentuated sway of Frenchy's young, slender hips as she followed Bob to the center of the dance floor. An unsettling bit of nausea gripped Pearl's stomach. Was it her overindulgence the past evening or the young, svelte body dancing with Bob? She reached for the champagne sitting in front of her. "Let's don't get started on this tonight," she told herself. She signaled the waiter, asked for a diet Coke, and watched Cherie's anorectic figure gyrate through the dance.

The music stopped as the waiter placed the Coke in front of her. The band started playing "Night and Day." Jacques met Cherie before she and Bob cleared the floor. Bob came to the table and extended his hand. "Are you ready for another?"

Nervously, Pearl sipped the coke and quickly surveyed the ballroom. Several couples graced the floor and more were walking up. "I'll give it another try." She took his hand and rose.

He led her to the floor, guided her into the dance position, and, for two measures, counted beats, which helped Pearl get the beat. At precisely the correct moment, she instinctively followed his imperceptible lead.

She intuitively followed Bob through the first two patterns then, from her college days, recalled the foxtrot basic rules. Silently, she counted, "Back, back, side and side. Back, back, side and side." She lost the rhythm and stumbled, once over her foot, and once by stepping on his. "Sorry," she said.

"No problem." Bob gently stopped, let her regain her balance, again counted two measures, and patiently led off. Again, after the first graceful patterns, Pearl, wanting to get the steps just right, began counting. Again, she lost the beat, stumbled, and stiffened. This time Bob didn't stop, he just softly hummed the music, emphasizing the downbeat, and continued to guide her around the floor. She tripped several more times, supported herself on his sturdy frame, and never lost balance. Positive that she was a clumsy drag, she apologized each time. He always gave her a reassuring look, said no problem, and maintained a relaxed smile.

Finally, the music stopped. "Thank you, but I feel I'm a burden."

"You're no burden at all. It's just been a long time. I know the feeling."

"You do?"

"I haven't danced much since Sarah died. It feels good to be on the floor."

The strains to "Smoke Gets in Your Eyes" filled the air. "That's a nice, breezy foxtrot. Want to give it another shot?"

"Sure," Pearl said. "It's your feet."

Pearl mechanically blundered her way through to the end. Thankfully, the band took a break, and she and Bob settled at the table. The others in their party sat at the bar where Cherie, advertising her varicose-free legs, flirted with several men while Jacques and Mac, oblivious of the emaciated French consort's boredom, engaged in animated conversation.

The band returned, and Pearl botched, fumbled, and bungled her way through several more waltzes and foxtrots, silently promising that she would never again make such a fool of herself. After the final dance, she and Bob walked back toward the Creole. The moon showed brightly overhead. A cool breeze brushed her hair. She tucked the white shawl closer to her neck. "I really enjoyed the evening," she said. "Sorry I spoiled it for you."

"Oh, quite the contrary, I appreciate your being sport enough to be my dance partner. Thanks for the pleasant company."

She admired his kind manner. "Did my inexperience show?"

"Yes, but, I have to say, when I helped at the studio, I danced with many women. You are in the top 25 percent as far as natural potential goes."

The compliment warmed her. "Really?"

"Oh, yes. To enjoy dancing, it takes more than just the ability to move around the floor. Something people refer to it as the X-factor, that unknown element. I could tell that you experienced it several times this evening."

Pearl found herself feeling a bit uncomfortable with such a nice compliment from a man. When most of the men in her life complimented her, it usually meant they wanted something. Bob seemed different. She hoped he was. Yet a strange feeling penetrated her soul. "Probably because of you. Actually, I felt like an ox in a mud field."

"Well, you weren't. You were relatively smooth and graceful."

"Relative to what? A bull?"

Bob laughed. "You're being much too critical of yourself." They entered the Creole, walked into the Grand Corridor, and paused by the passageway leading to his room. "Could I get your address? Since I'm going to be down here rather frequently. Perhaps we can do this again?"

Pearl's heart leaped. "Of course, It's Pearl Johnson —"

Bob, fumbling through his pockets, interrupted, "Just a minute. I have to get a pencil and paper."

Pearl watched as he stepped into the dim passageway, opened the door to his room, and turned on the light. She peered into the room as he walked over to the telephone table and picked up a pad and pencil. He had a confident, unassuming air. She wondered what it would be like to be in a hotel room with a man. Guilt flooded her every pore. She was still a married woman! He returned. Anxiety gripped her.

"Pearl Johnson," he said. She regained her presence and gave him her address at St. Jude's. "You don't, by chance, have an e-mail address?"

"Why, yes we do. It's to me, stjude at acn two dot com." Bob jotted it down and repeated it. "Also, because of poor communications, we have a second, stjude at hotmail dot com."

Bob repeated all the information like the thorough businessman he was. "From these addresses it looks like everybody there can read your mail." He wrote as he talked.

"They can. And do. It's a small school. We only have one computer connected to the Internet."

He removed a sheet of paper from his pad and handed it to her. "Here's my address and e-mail. Maybe we can solve the computer problem."

She perked up and switched to her missionary-opportunist personality. "Are you serious?"

"Sure. I have many friends that have old but perfectly good computers they'd be willing to donate to a good cause."

"We only have two. We could easily use four more." Anxiously, she pushed her luck. "And good UPS systems to go with them."

"Of course. Would some laptops be sufficient?"

Pearl's anxiety level skyrocketed. "Oh, yes. Particularly if we could get spare monitors and keyboards to accompany them."

"Next time I come down, I'll bring some laptops and keyboards. They're easier to carry. Perhaps we can purchase monitors locally. Maybe I can get some Rotary Clubs to help."

"That would be great!"

"Almost midnight," Bob said, glancing at his watch. "I've got an early start to a long day tomorrow. Can I walk you to your room?" As on the dance floor, he gracefully led her down the Grand Corridor.

"It isn't necessary."

"I know, but I did appreciate your company this evening so the least I can do is see you safely to your room."

Nerves alerted every molecule in her body. She wasn't sure what to expect. Was she getting herself into an awkward situation? Did she want to? As she led him up the narrow stairs, she fumbled for her key and wondered if he were comparing her fat hips to Frenchy's. They stopped in front of her door. "Here we are."

"Room three zero seven." He lifted her hand and kissed it. "Thank you for sharing a part of your life with me this evening. Good night." He abruptly turned and walked away without waiting for a reply.

Pearl unlocked and entered the empty room. A war of emotions raged. He had not tried anything, and she had been a klutz on the dance floor, regardless of what he said. Was he not interested? Did she not interest him? Was that an insult or compliment that he didn't make a pass? What could she have done? What *should* she have done? For the evening to come to such an abrupt halt, she must have done something wrong. And what had she wanted from the night out?

A warm bath didn't quell her conflicts. Still awake at two o'clock, she got up, walked to the pool, sat on the edge, and dangled her feet in the crystal-clear water. She looked at the moon, then gazed longingly through the dining room to the passageway leading to his room.

"This is childish," she said aloud, "utterly foolish." She kicked the water and watched the spreading ripples shatter the reflecting moon. Finally, tiredness set in, and she returned to her room. The last thing she recalled was the red letters on the clock reading five minutes past three.

Moland's Bull Session

Michelette's Awakening

Monday morning, Michelette walked up to Francois's compound. Embedded in the center of the wrought-iron gate was a creamy ceramic tile sign with multicolored lettering saying "La Petite." She picked up a discarded plastic orange juice bottle, lifted the padded hammer from its cradle, and gently tapped the suspended three-foot diameter brass Chinese-style gong.

"Yes?" came Francois's voice from the speaker.

"This is Mikey. Can I talk to you for a little bit?"

"Sure. Come on in."

The electric lock snapped, and the heavy gate swung open, its cast-iron hinges noisily objecting. When the opening was large enough, Michelette squeezed through and pressed a red and a white button mounted on the wall. The gate clunked to a stop, then reversed direction.

"We're at the table," Francois called as Michelette tossed the bottle in a red, white, and green striped fifty-five gallon oil drum that served as a trash can. She waited for the gate's latch to set, then Michelette walked down the drive, rounded the corner of the house, and saw the artist and Georges at the table, coffee mugs in hand and empty plates on the table.

"Hi," Georges said, rising and picking up the dirty dishes. "Nice to see you, but I know you didn't skip school this morning just to see me. Care for some coffee?"

"No, thank you," Michelette said.

"How about some coffee cake and milk?" Francois asked.

"I'd like that."

Georges walked toward the house. "I'll bring it out."

Michelette watched, and when Georges disappeared through the door, she turned to Francois. "I'm sorry to interrupt your time with him, but I had to talk to someone, and Mrs. Johnson isn't at school today."

"That's all right, Mikey. I gather you didn't have a very good weekend."

"It was horrible. Mama and I didn't say much at all." Michelette pulled a neatly folded piece of paper from her backpack.

Georges came out with a loaded tray, set a piece of cinnamon coffee cake and a glass of milk in front of Michelette, refilled Francois's mug, and picked up his cup. "I'll leave you two alone."

Michelette looked at him. "Thanks. I'll only be a few minutes."

"No problem, young lady. Take your time." The women again watched Georges go into the house.

"He's really a nice man," Michelette said.

"Sure is. Now, what's up?" She scooted closer

"I thought a lot about the test and mama. I know I hurt her, hurt her bad." Michelette explained what happened. "I couldn't sleep much. So I wrote and wrote and wrote. I tried to draw and couldn't. Only words came out. And this," she unfolded the paper, "is what I ended up with, and I wanted you to read it to see if it made sense. It does to me, and I guess that's most important, but I want to know if you think what I say is right or wrong because I'm not very good with words. I hope they paint the picture that is in my heart. I used my old dictionary, but I don't think all the words are right." Michelette handed the paper to Francois, who read silently. The teenager carefully studied the artist's expression.

Finally, Francois looked at Michelette. A tear in each eye twinkled. Francois reread the poem. A slight tremble shook the page. "Mikey, this is beautiful. It's as much a work of art as a picture. You have wonderfully depicted a timeless universal condition." She turned and called, "Georges, would you come out here a minute?"

"Francois!" Michelette said, almost panic-stricken.

"You don't mind, do you? I think he will appreciate it as much as we."

"But I'll be embarrassed. You know, the test!"

"This," Francois said, waving the paper, "isn't just about the test. This is about living today."

Georges walked out, mug in hand. "What is it?"

"I'd like for you to hear something Mikey has written."

Georges straddled the bench and sipped his coffee. "I'm all ears."

Francois read aloud.

Yesterday's Traditions

Tribes in the ancient land,
Lived as necessary to survive.
The community, they were told,
Was more important than a single soul.

Perceived necessities of the time
Became religious rituals of yesteryear.
But as living requirements take new form,
Should not past religious conventions reform?

In this place and at this time,
For mankind to remain whole,
Is it possible that, for civilization to survive,
The most important element be the individual soul?

Old traditions carry strong measure,
Especially to those for whom they buttress,
But for us whom the ancient customs pain,
Is it truly necessary that old practices remain?

As a child of many generations,
I honor those who came before me.
Their soul may find comfort in their tradition,
To refuse happiness to their spirit is not my ambition.

My elders deserve contentment,
To oppose that is not my intent.
But how I react to their ancient convention
Is, no matter how difficult, in my time and space
dimension!

When she finished, Georges took a deep breath and exhaled. "Wow! That's strong stuff." He looked at Michelette, then Francois, and back to Michelette. "Read it again."

As Francois read, Georges stared at Michelette. She could tell from his expressions that he knew what this was all about. Her stomach wrenched. She just knew that he was going to say something that would embarrass her. When Francois finished, he took another sip, set the mug on the table, and looked into Michelette's eyes. She prepared herself.

"You're right, young lady," he said. "We have no control over what happens to us, but we do have control over our reactions. My strongest fight isn't with the businessmen, the fish, or Mother Nature; it's overcoming the attitude that whatever happens is God's will and therefore must be good. The old bondye bon philosophy. And this writing," he said, "hits that problem right on the head."

Michelette relaxed and looked at Francois. "So you think that it's okay if I show that to Mrs. Johnson? You think she will understand?"

"I think Mrs. Johnson would be proud."

"What about Mama?"

Francois paused. "That, I believe, is up to you. She may understand it, and she may not. Sometimes people who are so involved in day-to-day existence cannot recognize an issue even if it is clearly spelled out like this. Perhaps it would be best if you asked Mrs. Johnson that question. She has children. I don't."

Michelette felt better. Though it took her all weekend to write the simple poem, the process helped resolve her conflict. Because of their strong mother-daughter bond, she would not resist the test, but resolved not to allow it to affect her as it had in the past, and she promised herself that if she ever had a daughter, she would not continue the practice. Pleased with herself, she stood. "Thanks. Now I've got to go. I'm already way late."

"I'll take you," Francois said.

"I'll tag along," Georges suggested.

Moland's Interest

Pearl slept late. She awoke refreshed, yawned, and stretched. Then, with both hands supporting her head, she relaxed in bed reminiscing about the prior evening. Leisurely, she got up, showered, dressed, packed, and went for a late breakfast. Thankfully, even though it was almost ten o'clock, the buffet was not too picked over.

Only three empty tables remained. At one shaded table sat the French surgeon, reading a manual, and his girlfriend, wearing a pink see-through lace cover over a skimpy white bikini. Her bored eyes wandered. She spotted Pearl, nonchalantly waved, and smiled. Pearl, thankful that they were at a table for two, returned the gestures.

She set her purse on a small, half-shaded table, then studied the buffet more closely than at first pass. A waiter asked her if she'd like coffee. She pondered for a moment. "Iced mango tea, please. And toast." The waiter nodded. She selected a plate, chose some fresh cantaloupe, papaya, and melon, then returned to her table and sat on the shaded side. Moland would be along sometime within the next two hours so she had plenty of time.

Before the waiter brought the tea, out of the corner of her eye she saw the pair from France rise. The surgeon spotted her and headed over. The bombshell's so-called cover-up didn't. Pink high heels magnified every muscle in her cellulite-free legs and accented her hip sway. Almost all diners' eyes followed as she trailed the doctor.

"Good morning," he said. "Did you enjoy last evening?"

As Pearl returned the salutation, Thom, the popular waiter, walked up carrying a box about the size of a small vase, an envelope taped to it. "Pardon me, Ms. Johnson," he said, looking at Pearl. "Mr. Turner asked me to give this to you."

"Thank you." Curiosity brewed as she took the box. Thom nodded and walked away.

"Well," the surgeon said, "it looks as if you did have a good time." His girlfriend gazed at the box.

Pearl felt herself blush. She started to tell him that nothing happened to warrant a gift but chose not to. "It was a lovely evening. Did you enjoy it?"

"It was okay. I'm not much of a dancer. We'll leave you to your breakfast. Hope to see you again sometime."

"And both of you," Pearl replied.

Silence overtook the dining area until the pair was out of sight, then envious and embarrassed chuckles arose as if from a classroom of murmuring children during certain health education movies.

Pearl removed a note from the envelope and unfolded it. "Thanks for a lovely evening," it said. "I saw this on display this morning and thought you might like it. Will be in contact about the computers soon." Bob had signed it. She opened the box and removed a small brown wood carving portraying a man and woman dancing, the woman's full skirt swirling. The warm feeling again engulfed her.

Just as she finished her fruit, Moland ambled up to the table and took a seat. "How was Wayne?"

"Just fine. And your weekend?"

"The usual." He signaled for the waiter. "Held a meeting just outside Jacmel. Spent most of the weekend on the beach at Bainet." His eyes bored into Pearl's.

"What are you looking at?"

The waiter approached, and Moland asked for coffee. "Anything else?" the waiter asked. "Toast perhaps?"

"No, thank you," Moland replied. "Just coffee. Put it on her bill."

Pearl nodded. When the waiter walked away, Moland said, "You had a very good weekend, and I don't think it was all Wayne."

"What makes you say that?" His clairvoyant gaze hurt her eyes. She nervously glanced over his shoulder at a pair of birds stealing breadcrumbs from the remains of an unfinished breakfast.

"Your expression. It's something I haven't seen before in you. Did you meet someone?"

"You're guessing, aren't you?"

Moland smiled. "The eyes are a pathway to the soul, and down that road I see a soul stirred by confused happiness. Only another person can do that. Are you about ready?"

She wondered what there was about this wizened old man. Could he really see into her soul? Was she that transparent? "After we finish coffee."

They stopped at the bookstore and picked up the proofs to Pearl's story, a box of pencils for Sister Joan, and twenty composition books for Sister Marie. She paid for the proofs herself, but put the supplies on charge. The bookstore seldom gave credit, but the owner had graduated from St. Jude's.

On the way home, after they cleared the heavy traffic, Moland said, "So, tell me about the man."

"What man?" Pearl asked while looking out the window at the piles of broken, crushed glass along the roadside. "That colored glass could be used at school to make mosaics. And I'll bet Francois could come up with some other ideas."

"So do I, but don't change the subject. You know what man."

"It was no big deal," Pearl said, defending herself when she didn't need to.

"Pearl. I see the radiance. Have you been keeping something from us? Was this a clandestine meeting?"

"Moland!" She playfully slapped his arm. "You nosy old buzzard. It's none of your business." She longed to tell someone, but suppressed her excitement. What she really would like was an old-fashioned slumber party with several giggling high schoolers. "I did meet a man, and we danced some last night."

"And he lit up your spirit."

The Voduan shaman's perceptiveness amazed her. "Now you're not going to say anything back at school, are you?"

"Now, Pearl," he said, feigning hurt.

His quiet, penetrating intellect reached into her heart and pulled out the story. She proceeded to tell, in infinite detail, all about the weekend, from stumbling into Bob on Friday to the dance on Sunday, including her sleepless night. By the time she finished describing the weekend's events and answering Moland's occasional question, they were pulling into the school compound.

"I'd like to continue this discussion tonight," Moland said. "Think you're up to a barnstorming session with Francois and Father Mike?"

"I think so. The usual time?"

"Yes."

Pearl looked forward to their sessions. Often they were light, but occasionally they delved into complicated philosophical subject matter. Tafia flowed freely, but not excessively. Usually, while interesting, the discussions regarding religion, mythology, philosophy, poetry, and art exceeded Pearl's understanding, but unknown forces most often kept her pinned to her chair.

The Meeting

After dinner, Pearl and Father Mike walked along the path to Moland's. "So, how was Wayne?" the priest asked, shooing flies from his face.

"He's fine." She briefly summarized the weekend.

Father Mike O'Shaughnessy was a particularly easy person with whom to talk. He was thirty-five years old, born of Irish immigrant parents in Cleveland, Ohio, had flaming red hair and pure blue eyes. Freckles accentuated his youthful look and helped hide an uncharacteristically deep wisdom. He was the youngest of five and the only one in his family called to the priesthood. One summer in high school he had helped a group of young people construct a school

113

building near Cap Haitian. When in a Dublin seminary, he voiced a strong desire to return to Haiti. The Church gave him his wish and assigned him to St. Jude's ten years earlier where, over time, he became fluent in Creole and passable in French.

"Well, you certainly came back looking refreshed, relaxed, and in bright spirits," Father Mike said. "More so than other times." He ducked under a drooping palm frond, then held it for Pearl.

"Thank you." She stooped under. "Have you been talking to Moland?"

"No, why?"

"Well, I did meet a man —"

"Oh, oh. Do we have something to confess?" An impish grin crossed his boyish face. She fell in behind him as green shrubs crowded the path. A small lizard darted across, chased by a larger one.

"I don't, Son," Pearl replied, "Do you?" She felt maternal toward Father Mike, yet respected his unique wisdom.

"Touché."

She briefed the priest on Bob Turner, including the promise to help out with computers. She chose not to tell him about her confused feelings.

"Don't hold your breath on the computers or anything else," Father Mike said. "As you know, it's easy for people to come down here, see or hear the needs, and promise more than they can deliver. More often than not, when they go back home, their conscience will be bothered for a while, but most seldom follow through."

"I don't think that'll be the case here."

"Besides, you'd like to see him again?"

"Father. I'm a married woman." Her silent answer was yes.

"Unhappily married, but married."

"Are you implying something?"

"No. Just making an observation."

They strolled into the clearing, dodged Francois's Suzuki, and walked around back where they figured Moland would be. Francois, her hair down, wearing a pink halter and short Levi cutoffs, held a brown pottery cup. She stood beside Moland. Georges, in tight khaki pants and blue denim shirt, the top two buttons unfastened, was in front of them with a yellow half-full glass. "Well," Moland said, "just in time to sample a freshly opened, ah, masterpiece of cane creation." He held up the three-quarter-full jug of clear liquid. "A very secret potion with special, magical powers!"

"I'll have a bit," Father Mike replied, accepting a small clear jelly jar into which Moland poured a hefty shot. "And what vintage might this so-called magical potion be?"

Moland sniffed his small blue glass, took a sip, and smacked and licked his lips. "I'd say a week-old ninety-nine, distilled using only the finest cane stalks of Point St. Marc and some secret cabalistic ingredients by the only true magician on this side of the Atlantic."

"Modest, aren't we?" Pearl said, accepting a surprisingly beautiful cobalt blue tumbler. "Any bat wings?"

"Bat wings are used only in fairy tales, my lady, and that is no ordinary glass," he said, filling it. "It yields mystical powers to those of pure thought who partake from it!" He refilled his own glass, then Francois's and Georges's. "It's awfully difficult to be both honest and modest!" He opened the door with his foot. "Let's go inside. I have a good feeling tonight."

Candles on the altar flickered. The smoky fragrance of incense filled the room. Moland did not immediately follow them in. The Voduan priest stood at the door facing outward, spread his arms, the jug in one hand and glass in the other, and raised his face skyward. "Bondye Gros Bon. Nèg di san fè, Bondye fè san di."

He turned to the group, who, in unison, repeated the Creole prayer in English. "God is very good. Man talks without doing, God does without talking."

Moland set the jug in the middle of the table and took his chair.

Francois sat across from Pearl, Georges to her left, Father Mike to the right. Moland's chair bordered the dance floor. "Well," Father Mike said, "what shall we talk about tonight?"

"A difficult subject came up this past week," Moland said. "Let's give love and hate a try."

"How about Michelette's charcoal?" Francois asked as she dipped a spoon of brown sugar from the cup at table's center, put it in her glass of spirits, and stirred. "It had love and hate portrayed in it."

"That young lady is something else," Moland said approvingly.

"Yes," Francois replied. "As a matter of fact, she should be among us. She is truly a bright child, one of the universe."

"Maybe she should be here instead of me," Pearl said.

"Why not you?" Father Mike asked.

"I don't feel much like a child of the universe."

"You," Moland said, "are more so than any of us."

"Why?" Pearl asked.

"Simple," the Vouduan priest responded. "You are not only a female, the vehicle of life in the world's process; you are mother for all time, and the only mother among our little group." He swept his extended arm over the table.

"Besides," Francois added, "you bring a special knowledge, that of parent-child love from the parent's view, and that's something for discussion. In Michelette's painting, love and hate existed side by side. Can that also exist in the parent-child relationship?"

Pearl thought of her conflict with Beverly. She loved Bev. Did Bev both love and hate her? How was that possible? "I'm afraid talking about love and hate together is too much for me. It's either one or the other, but existing together?" She thought back to her own childhood. Did she love and/or hate her father? Ted? "To be honest, in all my years, I've never given much thought to love. Naturally I love my children, and at one time, I suppose I loved my husband. But I don't see how love and hate can exist together."

"Well, let's see," Moland said. "Did you love your husband, or were your hormones calling for his?"

Pearl looked inside herself. She didn't like being the subject of conversation, and she was uncomfortable recalling her past. She felt as if her feelings were on trial. It was like her last few conversations with Beverly. Her defensives went on alert. "I really don't recall how I felt." She wanted to shift the conversation away from her. "How about you, Georges? What do you think of love?"

"It's a complex subject, but to me, it can't be stifling. It's very forgiving." He touched Francois's hand. "I know I love this lady."

"That's why a discussion about love in this small group is fine," Father Mike interjected. "Only clowns delve deeply into such complex subjects. We're among friends. And we're all clowns. All of us have hidden faces."

"And, like it or not," Moland said, "we all dance to the tune of the universe. A toast," he lifted his glass, "to us clowns and the universe." They touched their glasses over the center of the table, then took a swallow.

"Anything else you'd like to say?" Father Mike asked, speaking to Pearl.

She envied Georges and Francois. She knew they deeply cared for each other with an intensity that was beautiful yet not suffocating. She looked at young Father Mike, who loved God but some questioned whether or not he loved the Church, which is why, some had said, that he would always be stuck in this small, remote parish that few other priests, if any, wanted. The sisters at St. Jude's had sometimes referred to him as too charismatic and not firm enough when it came to instructing the students in Church doctrine.

"I took care of my kids and husband," Pearl said. "I fed 'em, took care of 'em when they were sick, and was always cleaning up after 'em. You know, all the things a housewife and mother has to do. It takes love to do that."

Father Mike, in his understanding tone, spoke. "True. Very true. But I suspect that you, like most people, have so imbedded into your subconscious the third level of love that you can't see, much less go, beyond."

"Now I'm really confused," Pearl said. "What do you mean 'third level'? Love is love." She hesitated. "Isn't it?"

Francois intervened. "Some say there are at least five levels of love. The first is the rules level. Master to servant. No time for thought. Obey the rules. The Ten Commandments. The parent of the very young child, the child who has yet to be able to reason. And the second level is friend to friend. This is the group level. Communities. That of parent and child when the child is discovering the world. The 'don't do this because it upsets the social order' type love."

"Then comes the most accepted," Moland said. "The third level." He paused. "This level is similar to that of parent and child after the child has discovered the world and strikes out on their own. The parent has to love them enough to not only let, but, in many cases, make them go. Recognize the individual worth, not only the community. This is the determining level, and the summit for many."

He paused and sipped his elixir. "These three levels of love, regardless of god or gods, serve people's animal natures—health, wealth, progeny, victory, and so on. All animals participate in these three levels."

Father Mike sipped his tafia. "Many people, unfortunately, don't get beyond these levels. Often they're not encouraged to go to the next level. Quite a few, particularly in their spiritual lives, stay at the first level."

This was beginning to make some sense to Pearl. "Before we discuss these, what are the other levels?"

"Spouse-to-spouse," Moland quickly answered. "The first three levels exist in all of God's creatures. Best as we can tell, the forth level only exists in a few select species, we humans foremost among them. A very difficult level, but truly a great one. Males represent society, and females represent nature. Love at this level is, in essence, the wedding of society and nature; when two people come together and realize that they are part of something greater than themselves. Neither conquers the other. Both are equal. Woman is the activating principal; the men just follow along, struggling to find their own way in the social order in which they find themselves. At this level, lovers are forever bound to each other."

This was totally foreign. There was no question that she had never been "bound" to Ted. She was bound to the institution of marriage because the Church said to be otherwise was a sin. Yet Father Mike never once said that Francois and Georges were living in sin. Was this a conflict? "I'm almost scared to ask about the next level." She lifted the cobalt tumbler to her lips and took a long, soothing swallow.

"The fifth level is —" Father Mike paused, "illicit love."

"Illicit love?" Pearl asked. "You mean to tell me that all those women with whom Ted had affairs were expressing love of the highest order, even higher than spouse-to-spouse?"

"No," Francois said. "That's usually one organ yelling for another, the animal desire that's necessary for the survival of any species, not even at the first level."

"At the fifth level," Moland said, "we're talking of love that defies logic and social order. Love that breaks into the transcendent. It surpasses all else, including self and society. The love that society says is wrong, senseless, or careless. All else drops off at the onset of this magnitude of love. It's the love that makes a mother lift a car off her husband or child; that causes a soldier to throw himself onto a grenade to save his buddies. It's what makes a person who can't swim jump into a river to save a stranger." He looked at Francois and Georges. "It's the love that reigns supreme in the face of adversity. The love of the people dying rather than renounce their God or country. The love for Allah that sends Muslims on suicide missions against their enemies, or the love for their homeland carried by Japanese kamikaze pilots during World War II." He paused.

"How about love of another of the same sex?" Father Mike asked.

"Could be," Moland replied. "Isn't true love genderless?" His eyes bored into each person sitting at the table, then he raised his glass. "Before we continue, a toast to us clowns."

Pearl, shocked at Father Mike's suggestion, welcomed the break. To even consider that homosexual love might be of the highest order was a bit much. "Hear! Hear!" Still trying to clarify in her own mind the various levels of love, she wasn't sure she was ready for much more deep conversation. But she could no longer quell her quest for spiritual discovery. At last, she knew she had to find her own path, not the one set for her by the Church. She had to go down one never traveled. Was this a blessing or a curse?

"To us clowns!" The others said in unison.

Moland put down his glass and began patting the edge of the table with both hands in four-four time, emphasizing the downbeat. "Everybody. Let's get in touch with our clown self so we can relax. Unwind. Maybe think a bit freer. Set aside our social self."

Pearl set her glass on the table and began keeping rhythm on its edge with both hands. This was more like it. This was relaxing.

All four began keeping time with Moland. As the beat gathered steam, Moland closed his eyes and began nodding his head with the time. Pearl began to feel the rhythmic signals throughout her body. She felt her heart beating to the same cadence. Was this a coincidence?

Francois picked up her and Moland's spoons, and, to the beat, used them as a percussion instrument against the palm of her hand. Father Mike used his spoon on the edge of the glass. Everyone rocked or swayed.

Moland, his body undulating in time, rose and moved to the dance floor, clapping to the beat. Francois followed, keeping cadence with the spoons. She began to dance like a Spanish flamenco dancer, first clapping the spoons to her palm above her head, then at her waist. She swayed and arched like a tree sapling bowing with the wind. Moland moved close behind her clapping his hands above his head. Beads of sweat popped out on his forehead. Georges joined the pair. Moland, a conductor of life's orchestra, kept the beat. Father Mike pounded his feet. Georges and Francois, as if possessed by a demon, stared blankly at each other. Her hips rotated. Georges, never touching his soul mate, followed the contour of her body with his hands.

Suddenly, as if shocked by Georges's presence, Francois leaped and turned completely around, never missing a beat. Georges, perspiring heavily, yanked off his shirt, buttons flying. He threw it across the room. Francois picked up the cadence. Everyone followed her beat. She kicked off her shoes and threw the spoons aside, put her hands on her hips, and, as if offering herself to Georges, arched her back high and danced to him.

Moland, as if on a cue, backed off the floor. Francois's eyes rolled back in her head. She stood upright, then jumped and turned in midair, once again facing Georges. Sweat beaded on both of them. She spread her legs and leaned backward, inviting Georges to come close. Their bodies, gyrating to the music, didn't touch. Her hair swept the floor. She began a gentle chant in an unfamiliar tongue.

Pearl stared at Georges's glistening, muscular chest, then followed down the rippling muscles of his abdomen to the round bulge below his waist, which swayed in unison with Francois, never quite touching. Pearl's eyes followed their hips. She swallowed. Her breathing marched to the beat. A euphoric, animalistic spirit invaded her body and captured every sensual zone. Suddenly, she and Bob Turner were on the dance floor. What was happening? Was she flowing with the eternal music of the universe or just losing control of herself? She could feel everyone's eyes penetrating her, absorbing her feelings. She couldn't allow this. How could Father Mike allow such goings on? This was against the rules. This was sinful. Yet she was spiritually anchored to her space.

Francois raised and clutched her knees. Georges danced back, giving his lover space. Her chanting increased, as did the rhythm of the beat. She gradually slid her fingers up the insides of her thighs. Before they reached where her legs met, they moved to the outside, and rested on her hips. Georges's hand covered hers. She stood erect and opened her eyes.

Encouraged by an internal force, Pearl's body struggled to rise and join the dance, but the social rivets in her brain kept her pinned. She closed her eyes, the first line of defense at preventing outside influences from feeding her body's life force. Father Mike recited Ecclesiastes 3. The words ". . . A time to cry. A time to laugh. A time to grieve. A time to dance . . ." They were the same as those read by the sisters during her high school days, but the meaning tonight impregnated her soul. The drumming bore to her inner sanctums, spraying lightning bolts of fear. She pressed her hands to her ears. Her heart responded with the thundering of warm spirit-filled blood racing through her veins. The pain of her body's call to join the dance grew to an excruciating crescendo.

She leaped from the chair and ran from the cabin. She had stepped onto the path never traveled, and it terrified her. She stopped and leaned against Francois's car, her heart racing and lungs gasping. Her stomach churned with nausea. She bent over, ready for what could happen. It didn't. She sucked in the heavy, moist air. Then she straightened up. A giant, satisfying mass finally calmed her lungs' desire. Her heart slowed. Sweat dripped from her nose. Her dress clung to her body, and her skirt drooped heavy with perspiration. She stared at the moon, wondering what had come over her.

Father Mike shuffled up. "Are you okay?"

"I'm not sure."

"What happened?"

"I don't know." She took another deep breath. "If I didn't know any better, I'd say I was scared. More scared than I have ever been."

"Scared?"

"Yes. Like something was trying to possess me. Something evil." She began to shiver.

She crossed her arms and hunched her shoulders.

"Are you sure it was something evil?"

"I can't think of anything else that would cause me to feel like this."

"Perhaps it was a call to quit worrying about yesterday and tomorrow and begin living today. I believe it was Jesus who said something like that, that one should live one day at a time and not worry about yesterday, for that is past, or tomorrow, for God will provide. Maybe Pearl Johnson's spirit is telling her to join the march of time and dance the rhythm of living today."

"I don't understand," Pearl said, shivering in the sweltering heat of the night.

As a father would his daughter, Father Mike put his arm around Pearl's shoulders and walked with her toward St. Jude's. "I'm reminded of a story that exists in many different mythologies. It's about a wolf that is raised by a herd of sheep. It seems that a lone, starving, pregnant, female wolf —"

"Wolves are social animals," Pearl said, interrupting.

"This is my story," Father Mike said, smiling. "Anything is possible. Please let me finish."

"Okay."

"The very weak and pregnant wolf sees a herd of sheep. She pounces, trying to catch one, but they scatter, and the effort causes her to give birth to three pups, immediately after which the wolf dies, along with two of the pups. The sheep, being the nurturing animals they are, adopt the living pup and begin to raise him as a sheep. The pup drinks sheep's milk, and he grows, acting as much as possible like the other lambs in the herd. When it comes time for him to graze, he tries, but can't, because he doesn't have the proper teeth. Just before he is finished weaning, a lone male wolf pounces among the sheep, who scatter, leaving the skinny, hungry pup, who is still trying to eat grass. Not being a sheep, he's not afraid. The big wolf looks at the pup and asks, What are you doing, trying to eat grass? The pup, staring wide-eyed at this big thing in front of him, bleats like a sheep, and says that he's trying to eat because he's hungry. Well, says the big wolf, you need to eat wolf food because you're a wolf, not a sheep. The pup looks puzzled. The big wolf grabs the little pup by the neck, takes him to a clear puddle of water, makes him look at the two reflections, and tells him, 'See, you're not a sheep. You look like me! You're a wolf! You need to eat like a wolf!' He takes the pup to his den, where he has the remains of an antelope, and shoves a piece down the pup's throat. The pup immediately chokes and spits the meat out. But the big wolf shoves it in again and again until the pup finally swallows it. Then the nourishment spreads through his body, and he feels good, he feels more like the wolf he really is." Father Mike paused.

"Okay. So what's the point?"

"After living a false life, or a life programmed by others, we often choke when we encounter our true doctrine, or nature."

Father Mike's parable did little to settle her down. Just this past Thursday, she was very comfortable and satisfied with her life and status. Now her emotions were in turmoil. Her insides shook, her brain spun, and her heart ached. She longed for the simple life of rules. Yet her very being told her she could never go back.

She had started down her own path.

They walked to St. Jude's in silence. As Pearl thought back, it had all begun when she tripped at la Villa Creole. How could stumbling over a dumb computer case lead to such misery? What was it going to take to cure her pain?

Back at her refuge in the Nest, she tossed until daybreak.

The Vision

Pearl and the Poem

Tuesday after class Pearl sat at her desk, a small stack of compositions in front of her. She underlined a word, then glanced up to watch a butterfly light on a pink hibiscus just outside her window. The events of the past few days made it difficult for her to concentrate. Her mind was in turmoil.

A gentle knock took her attention from the colorful insect to the partially open classroom door where Michelette stood, her backpack tucked under her arm, a sheet of paper in hand.

"Come in," Pearl said, "How are you?"

"I'm fine." Michelette walked over. "May I talk with you?"

"Of course." Pearl laid her red pencil aside. "Anything in particular?"

Michelette looked down at the floor and shuffled her foot, brushing aside any lingering hesitation.

"Let's sit over here," Pearl said, rising and going to a pair of armchair desks by the window. She turned one so the two of them would face each other. Both sat.

"Mrs. Johnson," Michelette stammered and hesitated. "Has anyone ever told you about the test?"

Pearl thought for a moment and wondered if one of the sisters had given a particularly difficult exam. "What test?"

Michelette shifted uncomfortably, looked around, and then murmured, "The virginal test."

Pearl, after learning that she had been accepted to teach at St. Jude's, had researched Haiti and its traditions. One of her references had mentioned the test, but she assumed that the practice had long been discontinued. "I've heard about it, but it's not done anymore, is it?"

Michelette raised her eyebrows and looked out the window. A hummingbird hovered at the mouth of the hibiscus blossom. She nodded.

"Oh, my goodness. I had no idea."

Michelette began telling about her mother performing the tests. As she spoke, her eyes wandered. While following the flight of a black and yellow butterfly flitting from flower to flower, she told of her conversation with Francois on Friday. On the windowsill, two geckos danced through their mating ritual as Michelette explained the encounter with her mother this past Friday night. Then looking at the cursive English alphabet above the chalkboard, she rambled through the enduring weekend and explained Monday's visit with Francois and Georges. When she finished, she handed Pearl the sheet of paper. "I wonder if you think I should show this to my mother."

As Pearl read the title, she wondered why, in these modern times, such an archaic rule could be perpetuated. She knew she had to handle this delicate situation with care. She read the poem, looked up and saw Michelette staring wide-eyed at her, then reread the poem. Pride that only a classroom teacher could feel welled up within. This was the work of one of her students. "Michelette, this is beautiful. I'm not sure what to say."

"I thought that you, being a mother, might be able to give me some advice."

"Like what? I don't think I can improve on this. It came from your heart."

"Should I show it to my mother?"

The question was loaded. Pearl thought back to her own childhood and wondered if she would have shown something like this to her mother. The answer was a quick no. Her mother never even broached the subject of monthly periods. Such topics were taboo. Would she have wanted her own children to bring up something like this? She struggled, but couldn't recall her children ever asking such questions. She wasn't sure how she would have felt, and was that in itself a failing of her as a parent? "I'd like some time to think about it. Would it be okay if we talked again after class tomorrow?"

"I suppose," Michelette answered, looking at the floor.

Pearl stood and put her hand on Michelette's shoulder. "I just want some time. I think this matter is too important to bring to resolution in just one sitting. Do you understand?"

"Yes, ma'am."

"May I keep this? I'd like time to study it more thoroughly."

Michelette's eyes sparkled. "That copy is for you. Do you really like it?"

"Yes, I really like it. It's a work of art. Will you sign and date it for me?"

"Sure," Michelette replied. She pulled a pencil from her backpack and signed and dated the document. "Same time tomorrow?"

"Yes."

Michelette left, and Pearl sat back down. She tapped her fingers on the desk and stared at two butterflies performing their instinctive aerial mating ritual. Her mind flitted to the religious sects that still practice circumcision, both male and female. Why was it that such religious rules were perpetuated? To outsiders, these rules were senseless, but to those who believe in such rituals, they're vitally important. Her stomach twitched. Something inside her wasn't right.

The Beach

Pearl reread the poem, tapped her pencil on the desk, twirled her hair, and reread it again. This ingredient, combined with the events of the past few days, served to make her brain a mixing bowl of confusion. There was no chance of her concentrating on the students' compositions. She neatly stacked the papers, smoothed the stack's edges, tucked them in a large envelope, and, carrying Michelette's verse rolled in her hand, walked over to the Kitchen. She found Natti whipping a bowl of batter.

"I'd like to make a sandwich to take out to the beach. Any suggestions?" she asked while stealing a finger-full from the bowl.

With the wooden spoon, Natti playfully swatted at Pearl's hand. "You gonna be here for dinner?"

Pearl licked her finger. "Umm. Coconut cookies! No, I don't think so."

Natti shook her head, lifted a dollop of batter, and allowed it to slowly plop back into the bowl. Satisfied, she set the bowl on the counter and wiped her hands. "You not eat right if I not cook for you. You go to your room. I fix something and bring it."

"I don't want to cause you any trouble, Natti. I'll fix it."

"You cause me trouble if you mess up my kitchen. Now go on." Natti shooed her on as she would a flock of chickens. "I make you something good and bring it."

Pearl left, her brain being stirred much like the batter in Natti's bowl. The past few days had brought up many issues. First she tripped over the computer case and something inside her flipped. Then her discussion with Wayne, and her attempt at a letter to Beverly. The pleasant yet upsetting dances with Bob Turner. Moland's comments about her eyes being the pathway to her soul. Then last night's session. The five levels of love. And now Michelette's poem. How could so many complex subjects come together in one person in such an uncomplicated place. Until this weekend, life had been simple.

In her room, she rolled together a light and heavy blanket. Just before the final tuck, she grabbed a towel and joined it to the roll. As she finished, she heard a tap on the door.

Natti entered and smiled as she lifted the blue cover from the brown palm basket and pointed out its contents. "A chicken sandwich, a thermos of iced tea, a little cup of fried banana slices, two cookies, a fork, and a napkin." Her inquisitive eyes looked at Pearl as she set the basket on the table. "You goin' out for some quiet time?"

"Yes. I imagine I'll be back by ten. Thanks for the food."

"My pleasure, Miss Pearl. You very nice lady." Natti paused at the door and looked toward the hazy sun hanging lazily in the western sky. "Ain't nature grand?"

"Yes," Pearl said, surprised at Natti's observation. It was the first time she had heard the culinary elder make such a comment.

"Ain't no way people can make it better. They only mess it up." Natti shuffled off.

Pearl, the blanket roll under one arm and basket in hand, walked out the back gate, up the beach and found her favorite spot under a coconut palm near the point. In the east, she could see the glow of lights from the town of St. Marc. To the west the sun was about to drop into Caribbean. Several people walked the beach. Some children played in the surf. Two couples sat near the water's edge watching the sunset. She envisioned Francois and Georges dancing across the horizon, just under the setting sun. Natti's closing words echoed in the wind.

At the base of the tree, she spread the heavy blanket, weighted a corner on the windward side with the picnic basket, and the other with her sandals. Warm tropical breezes gently blew through the palm fronds, creating sounds like artists' brushes on canvas. Pearl sat on the blanket, rested her back against the tree, opened a folder, and reread Michelette's poem. She folded it, tucked it back into the folder, and watched the palm fronds dance to the rhythm of the wind. Wispy clouds, gradually changing from white to pink to lavender, glided across the sky.

Suddenly, like falling coconuts, the questions hit. Was she one of Michelette's ancients? Was she guilty of continuing outdated religious practices? Had cultural programming blinded her? Was she a victim of ancient traditions?

Buried in thought, she almost missed the sun's dip in the ocean. Just as it disappeared, a green aura appeared for about five seconds. The flash of green! Legend had it that those who saw it would have a happy life. It was a beautiful wonder of nature, almost as breathtaking as Francois and Georges's love.

What about Francois's various levels of love? Transparent images of Francois and Georges danced in the clouds. Why had she run from the cabin rather than participate in the dance? Was she scared of her feelings? Was it a sin to want to participate? Who determined what was a sin? Which rules would be broken if she had jumped up and joined? Why hadn't Father Mike stopped the dance? Were traditions of old keeping Pearl stuck in one of the first three levels?

She glanced around the beach. Everyone had left but her. Solitude.

Father Mike's parable about the sheep and wolf cub. Was she choking on her truth? Was the comfort of rules keeping her from a fulfilled life? Was this what Beverly had been trying to tell her all along?

"One thing at the time," she told herself, speaking out loud. "I came out here to think about what I should advise Michelette." Pearl knew what a traditionalist would say, but she did not consider herself a traditionalist. She was a teacher, one who is supposed to help others in developing methods of finding the facts and truth.

But what was truth?

Why was life suddenly so complicated?

Knots gripped her stomach.

Perhaps a bite to eat would help. She opened the basket, pulled out and unwrapped the sandwich, lifted a corner of the homemade whole-wheat bread, and examined each piece of baked white meat. Light films of mustard. "Good for Natti. No mayonnaise." She bit into the sandwich, then laid it on the napkin, opened the thermos, and took a swallow.

A planet glowed in the west. In the east, a smattering of stars twinkled against the cobalt sky. Her mind wandered to the Beverly/Michelette persona. When Bev had brought up certain topics, Pearl recalled becoming defensive. A fence, or, better still, a wall had grown between them, one that had to be breached. How was she to advise the talented young artist? Was she even qualified? If Michelette brought this poem up to her mother, would it be the foundation of a wall?

Or, if the wall was already there, whose responsibility was it to tear it down? The question haunted Pearl because the answer was so obvious but hard to admit: in a mother/child relationship, it was the adult's responsibility. In other words, hers. That hurt!

But in the case of two adults, should it be a cooperative effort? How about Michelette's case? Michelette was a bright young lady. Who was the adult in her mother/daughter relationship? Would her mother retreat into the comfort zone of rules, or would she openly discuss the issue and come to a resolution that was fair to both?

Pearl took another bite of the sandwich. She noticed the lights of a jetliner moving across the sky. A sudden, gentle wind sent a brief chill throughout her body. She spread the light blanket over her legs as the moon peeked over the mountains. "By the Light of the Silvery Moon" played from memory as she watched the moon's reflection dance across Mud Crab Bay. She listened to the music of the wind and waltzed into drowsiness. Her eyelids, getting heavier, shifted to reverse blinks. . . .

A man and woman appeared from around the point, arms around each other's waist, strolling as one. She hoped they did not see her. She thought she knew them, but, in the twilight, couldn't be sure. She wanted solitude. But who were they? Definitely not Francois and Georges. Yet they were so very familiar.

Silhouetted against the moon's reflection, the couple stopped and kissed. A tinge of the same feeling Pearl felt the night before radiated throughout her body. Sensitive to the couple's privacy, she turned her head and looked to the horizon. She tried not to invade their realm, but curiosity finally won. She looked back, and the couple was in a passionate embrace. Pearl knew she should announce her presence, but the force said no.

Something within her, some power, an alien being maybe, demanded affection.

"What's wrong with me?" she wondered. She tried to get up. The force kept her pinned; her eyes locked on the couple. They parted. The man unbuttoned the woman's blouse, pushed it from her shoulders and allowed it to fall. He dropped to his knees, and, as Pearl's eyes magically zeroed in on the woman's glistening breasts, his tongue gently brushed each.

Pearl struggled to turn away, but couldn't. How could they have gotten so close without noticing her? Unconsciously, her fingers found her own nipples, then recoiled. But desire beckoned, and she didn't have the strength to resist. Her breathing deepened as she caressed her herself.

Suddenly she felt as if she were going to throw up. She yanked her hands away, clasped the round, firm thermos, and gulped, thirsting for the knowledge of life. Droplets of cool liquid trickled down and found the valley of her breasts. The wind and the waves pulsed to the rhythm of her heartbeat, a symphony that engulfed her body. The longing from her cradle of life beckoned as never before.

A male figure danced across the night sky.

The girl lay on the sand, the man over her. Their bodies slowly came together and, to nature's tempo, they moved as one.

Pearl's hand sought the ache beneath her skirt like a cautious explorer would blaze a new trail. She touched the point of yearning then recoiled as fast as she escaped from Moland's cabin the evening before. But, like the siren of the sea, the enchanting desire sang to her, and she listened. With fingers dancing to the rhythm of her universe, the music climaxed, and she responded with a spectacular, unknown, frightening, yet magnificent, applause. Her entire body, engulfed by a wave of euphoria, rejoiced. She moaned to the unfamiliar ecstasy, then, frightened by the new discovery, wailed like a terrified child.

She snapped open her eyes knowing that her involuntary cry would announce her presence to the couple on the beach. She scanned the shore. No one was in sight.

Palm fronds waltzed with the wind and waves embraced the shore. The evening breeze carried a nightbird's forlorn cry. Lightning streaked through a distant cloud. Emotionally exhausted, she lay her head on a rolled up towel, pulled the blanket to her shoulders, and fell into a deep sleep.

Eduardo's Glory

The Clinic

Franck St. Fleur, driving his Ford Explorer to St. Marc, asked Bob about his weekend. Bob told of his visit to Kenscoff, and the dance.

"Meet any interesting women?"

"Several. A young lady from France, two from Cuba, and one from the States."

Long before, Bob had concluded that Franck and his wife were genuinely concerned about his well being and had often expressed that everyone needs a mate. Bob found it very difficult to express his innermost feelings to anyone. During several brief conversations on this matter, he had not been able to convince his friend that the love of his life was still with him. He quit trying.

"All tourists, I assume?"

"All but the one from the States. She works here in Haiti. In a Catholic school. Somewhere up near St. Marc, I think she said."

"Which one?"

"I have it here somewhere." He reached into the back seat, pulled out his DayTimer, and fumbled through the loose papers.

"St. Martha's?" Franck asked.

Bob shook his head.

"St. Jude's?"

"I think that's it." He found his note. "Yes, St. Jude's."

"Is she a nun?"

"No. I think she said she had two grown children."

"Oooooh. Sounds like someone out to have a little bit of fun." Franck raised his eyebrows several times. "Any luck?"

Franck's insinuation was, of course, did Bob and Pearl end up in bed? This was the area in which Bob had more difficulty than any other expressing his point of view. With Sarah, sex was a sacrament that welded their marriage, delivering ultimate pleasure to both and creating three beautiful personifications of their love. Once sexual intercourse bridged the chasm from carnal knowledge to the complete bonding of body and spirit, there was no going back. Eros, in his purest form, had burned the bridge. Few men understood this concept, so Bob usually glossed over the issue. "Nope. She was a very nice lady." Deep inside, something murmured that this description was inadequate.

They rounded a curve and saw a tap-tap, hood up, stopped beside the road. A torso leaned over the fender, its head buried in the engine well of Haiti's most popular means of mass transportation. Several people stood off to the side. Franck pulled the Explorer over, and he and Bob walked back. A man, the apparent owner of the covered pickup, looked up as Franck spoke in Creole. The man, Franck explained, was futilely wishing a fan belt not to be broken. After a short discussion, he agreed to take the driver into St. Marc to get a new belt.

This said, most of the tap-tap's passengers drifted away, some into the bush, others down the highway. One, a skinny woman with a small child in a makeshift back carrier and a blanket role under her arm, just stood, despair emanating from her rusty, weathered face. After a bit of animated conversation, it turned out that she was taking her child to the Rotary Clinic to get his polio vaccine. She lived in a mountain village and had walked four hours to get to the road to catch a tap-tap. She feared that if she didn't get there today or tomorrow that she would be too late. Naturally, Franck offered her a ride. The woman wept with joy. Bob took the blanket and helped her and the baby into the utility.

The owner secured his tap-tap and climbed in behind Franck. As they drove toward St. Marc, the woman excitedly talked while Franck interpreted. She said that her village had heard about the polio vaccine over the radio, and that all the mothers in the village vowed to have their children vaccinated. Most had left two days earlier, planning to walk both ways, but she had saved enough money (about two American dollars) to be able to catch a tap-tap both ways, planning to overnight once beside the road.

It was mid-afternoon when they arrived at a roadside mechanic just outside St. Marc and asked about a fan belt. They followed his directions to an open-air parts kiosk under a mango tree. As the tap-tap owner got out, Franck asked, "Aren't you going to return the lady her fare?"

The driver, obviously embarrassed that he had been caught, fumbled in his pocket. "Of course," he replied. "Sorry. I forgot." He counted out sixteen gourdes. He turned to Franck. "Do I owe you anything?"

"No. Just do someone in need a favor someday."

After backtracking a few miles, they turned onto a rocky side road that eventually wound up the barren side of a hill toward a plateau where the clinic was. Franck had to stop twice while Bob shooed several goats off the road. A constant stream of women and children stepped aside to allow the vehicle to pass. Their passenger, upon seeing a group of women and children, excitedly rolled down her window and waved, then asked Franck to stop so she could get out. As she closed the door, she offered Franck the money the tap-tap driver had given her, but he refused. She thanked him profusely, almost to the point of embarrassment.

They reached the plateau and found it teeming with people. Franck pulled in beside Presley Dumas's truck. The compound's eight-foot-high white concrete-and-stucco wall had two door-sized gates, both open, and a secured vehicle entrance. In the blazing sun, a line of more than a hundred women slowly snaked its way into one gate while a steady stream of women and children exited the other. Hordes of children played games varying from hopscotch to tag, leaving their games only when called to go inside. One enterprising young man used his hands to propel himself and scooted along on a makeshift rolling personal platform faster than many of the children could run. Bob thought the scooter was playing a game until the young fellow with bright eyes and a captivating smile came close and Bob saw a pair of shriveled legs.

Franck and Bob paused for several minutes and counted. As twenty-two women and thirty-three children left the compound, thirty-one women and forty children joined the line, their former passenger, who smiled and waved, among them.

"This is the way all of the immunization programs are going," Franck said, wiping sweat from his forehead. "It's a problem just keeping enough vaccine flowing. And it has to stay refrigerated."

As Franck and Bob walked into the compound, two men carrying galvanized buckets of water came outside and were quickly surrounded by children. Bob and Franck waited for a third man, also carrying a water bucket, to exit and start down the line of women.

Inside the immunization building, Bob watched three physicians and several assistants administer the oral vaccine to the steady stream of children. Some balked, but most trustingly looked into the doctors' eyes, opened their mouth, and swallowed the drops. Almost without exception, the mothers closed their eyes with relief.

Presley stuck his head in the door. "A Kodak moment is here, Bob. The district governor just arrived." Presley served as escort for the small group, which included the compound's director as well as three other Rotarians and several people from the media. He explained the generator to the reporters, then started it. When it was up to speed, he threw the manual transfer switch and said that the whole compound was now on its own power. A grizzled man with a TV camera recorded the events as Presley led everyone to a well drilled with funds from a Rotary Club in Florida, the Rotary Club of Port-au-Prince, and Rotary International. "This is the first week that they haven't had to have water trucked in," Presley explained. He cupped some in one hand and drank it, then smiled as one of the Rotarians produced a stack of small paper cups. "Please help yourself."

Several small children looked on in amazement. Franck said that it was probably the first time they had ever seen water flowing from a pipe. He offered each child a cup. Most backed away, but one cute little brown girl with black eyes and a dimpled smile cautiously took one, looked at the water, then, as if asking permission, glanced back at Franck. He nodded, and she carefully put the cup under the flowing stream. It quickly overflowed and soaked her hand. She jerked the cup from under the water and, as only a scared child could, stared at Franck. The corners of her mouth drooped and her bottom lip trembled. Her eyes began to water. Franck smiled and winked, silently clapped his hands, knelt, steadied her little hand, and kissed her cheek. A person clapped. Gradually everyone joined the applause. Anxiously, the tyke's eyes darted around the crowd. The dimples returned, and her eyes glowed. She drank the water, handed the cup to Franck, then turned and ran to her friends. Again Franck offered the cups. This time all the children took one and got some water, each getting a little wet and rejoicing in every drop.

Bob looked around. Most all of the adults were wiping their nose. Then he saw the TV cameraman.

He, too, was crying. But he had captured the entire scene.

A Stroke of Good Fortune

Eduardo, Michelette's friend, sat in the bow of Domino's weather-beaten, paint-chipped sixteen-foot skiff, tenderly holding a hand line. Eduardo was good at bottom fishing, good enough to know by feel when a gentle snatch would set the hook. Domino, a full-blooded African, sat at the other end. No one, including Domino, really knew his age, but his leathered face and mouth of stained, rotting, snaggled teeth led one to believe that he was at least three times as old as the twenty-seven-year-old Johnson outboard that hung off the back of the boat. The wind was picking up, and the sea was a bit rough. Even though they only had two fish totaling no more than five pounds, neither liked rough water. And neither was a good swimmer.

Domino sniffed as he looked around, studying the water and air. His big nostrils quivered. "Better pull in," he said. "Don't like the air." He began winding his hand line around its plastic bottle reel.

"Okay." Relieved, Eduardo followed suit. A fish an hour wasn't good, but it was better than nothing.

As Eduardo hauled up the rock anchor, Domino yanked the Johnson's starter rope, and the motor sputtered to life. Eduardo laid the rock in its little well and pointed to a large white boat on the horizon. Domino, his floppy straw hat waving in the wind, glanced at the vessel and nodded. He made sure everything was secure, then pointed the bow toward shore. The little boat skimmed smoothly through the waves and approached the beach where he kept it tied.

Eduardo, holding a small hemp line, jumped out just before the bow touched shore and pulled the boat halfway up as Domino killed the engine. The old man suddenly stood up and looked at the tree line. Eduardo turned and saw a well-dressed man with a mustache, escorted by three other men, all cleanly dressed, walking toward them. Domino stepped out of the boat and met the lead man.

"Hello," the gentleman said, speaking Creole with a Spanish accent. "I'd like to rent your boat for a short time. I believe the going rate is two hundred dollars."

Eduardo was astounded. Two hundred American dollars was a lot of money. According to their agreement, Eduardo got 15 percent of the gross take, be it in money or catch. He couldn't figure out how much that was, but knew that Domino could. He yanked Domino's arm. "How many gourdes is that?"

Eduardo had never seen Domino's eyes get so big. He squatted, picked up a broken shell, scratched in the sand, then looked at Eduardo. "That's three thousand two hundred gourdes. Your share would be four hundred eighty."

That was more money than Eduardo had ever heard his mother talk about. Boy, would she be proud of him if he brought home that much. She could buy a new dress, and maybe he could get some store-bought candy. Maybe even a Coca-Cola. Who would have ever thought a day like today would turn into riches beyond his wildest imagination.

147

"Sir, we'd like to stay with the boat," Domino said. His eyes, a bit narrow, scrutinized the man. "Would you like us to carry you someplace?"

"We want to take some packages to the yacht just offshore," the man said, pointing.

Domino looked seaward and saw that the big boat had come much closer. He studied the water and wind, and scratched his wrinkled chin. "How big?" He pointed to his boat. "This is a little boat, and the water is rough."

The man snapped his fingers and pointed in the direction they had come. Two of his escorts went into the coconut grove and returned, each carrying two suitcases. They set them beside their leader and stood close as Domino tested the weight of each. Again the old man squinted seaward, scratched under his straw hat, then said, "That's only fifteen, maybe twenty minutes out. If we go now, we can do it in one trip. But the boat will not make it if we take all packages and a man. We can be quick if only my friend and I go."

The Spanish man pulled a little gray box from his pocket, looked at it, and punched it many times with his pointing finger. In Spanish, he talked to the box. After a few words, the man folded the box and put it back in his pocket. "That'll be fine."

"When do I get paid?" Domino asked.

The man reached in another pocket, pulled out a wad of money, counted out some, and handed it to Domino. "Here's half. The man on the boat will pay you the rest."

Domino nodded, stuffed the money in his only good pocket, picked up two suitcases, and motioned for Eduardo to get the other two. They carefully set the suitcases in the boat in two stacks. The top edge of each stack was about even with the top of the side of the boat. Eduardo pushed off to where only the bow was knee deep. The motor was in deep water. Domino yanked the starter rope while Eduardo held the bowline. On the second pull, the motor belched, sounded tired as always, but chugged to life. Domino nodded. Eduardo pushed hard and jumped in. Domino swung the bow around and headed out.

The sides of the boat were only a hand span above the waterline, but Eduardo knew that if Domino kept the bow into the waves there would be no trouble. Still, he watched to make sure no water was coming in. He was a little bit scared, but all that money was worth it!

The man on shore had called the big boat a yacht, a word Eduardo had never heard before. To him, it was a ship. He had never seen anything that big floating on water. Ten or fifteen boats as long as Domino's would fit on it, and it looked like it had two big houses stacked on top. A bunch of little round windows was all lined up on its side. And that big anchor would sink their little boat. On the ship's highest point, a little thing about as long as a paddle turned round and round. Beside it a small cup spun like crazy. And Domino had to dodge a stream of water shooting from a pipe sticking out the big boat's side.

A man in light blue pants and white shirt, wearing what looked like a black soldier's hat, lowered some steps with maybe ten flat boards on the end. When the thing stopped moving, the man came down, stood on the boards, and motioned for them to come alongside.

They did, and without standing up Eduardo, one by one, handed the man the suitcases, and he passed them to another man at the top of the steps. The man in the blue jacket was very polite, said thank you in French, handed Eduardo a roll of money, then went back up the steps. Eduardo passed the money to Domino. As Domino turned the boat toward shore, the steps went back up, and the ship's motors rumbled. White water boiled up from the ship's back end, and it gradually turned and headed out under the afternoon sun.

When Eduardo and Domino reached shore, the men were gone. After securing the boat, Domino counted all the money, then counted aloud as he handed Eduardo his share. The closer Domino got to four hundred eighty, the more Eduardo's hands shook. He had never in his life held so much money. His insides started to jump. He started giggling. "I'll go home now, Domino. I have to give this to Mama. Weren't we lucky today?"

A wide grin showing just how few teeth Domino had finally crossed his craggy face. "Many of my friends have had this same kind of luck," the old man said, his eyes glistening. "I never thought it would happen to me. Now I can take a day or two, maybe a week, and fix my boat." He patted Eduardo on the shoulder. "Now you go home. I'll come get you when I need you."

Running, skipping, and jogging, it took Eduardo more than an hour to get home. He raced into the house, handed his mother the money, and announced proudly, "This is what I earned today."

His mother looked at the wad and counted it out. "How did you make this?"

He explained the afternoon, including coming in early because the wind was kicking up.

"What was in the suitcases?"

"I don't know. Don't care. Clothes, I guess. The people were very rich."

"I'm proud of you, son." She counted the money again, then sat down. Tears rolled from her weary eyes.

"I'm going to tell Michelette." He bounded out of the house and ran down the path, eager to meet his friend and to tell her the story and to tell her that it was a good thing he wasn't in school today or he would have never made that money.

Michelette's Encounter

Michelette tapped on the door. Mrs. Johnson, standing by the window staring out, glanced around and motioned her in. Michelette ambled over and stood beside her teacher. Not knowing exactly how to open the conversation, she also stared out but couldn't find whatever it was Mrs. Johnson saw. Finally, she asked, "What are you looking at?"

Mrs. Johnson put an arm around Michelette's shoulder and pulled her close. "My past, Michelette." Mrs. Johnson again turned and stared out the window. "I was watching me as a little girl, then as a parent to my daughter, Beverly." Mrs. Johnson wearily lowered herself onto the nearest chair. "Please sit." She motioned to an adjacent desk. "I recall having things I wanted to talk about to my mother but couldn't. I just went along with the rules she set down. Then I grew up and became a parent to a very pretty, bright girl. I now know that she had many things she wanted to talk to me about. The only difference between her and me was that she did talk. I thought I listened, but your poem said to me that I only heard her words, not what she said. I refused to listen, to truly understand, probably because I was comfortable with my traditions and was afraid of what she was saying." She pulled a hanky from a pocket in the front of her dress and wiped her nose. "The true meaning of your poem awakened in me, a mother and old lady, some past ghosts and parental actions that no doubt had the same effect on my children as testing has had on you."

Michelette lowered her head in sorrow. "I apologize if I hurt you. I didn't mean to."

"Oh!" Mrs. Johnson exclaimed, patting Michelette's hand. "No apology is necessary. You didn't hurt me. You helped wake me up, and I'm happy you did." She paused. "The poem's like any great literature. It is supposed to stimulate something in the reader." They both watched a blue-green gecko scamper up the wall. "One problem with parenting," Mrs. Johnson said, "is that a person gets only one chance to be a parent to a given child. And parents, like any other humans, make mistakes."

"So am I making a mistake?"

"No. You are not."

"And my mother? Is she making a mistake, or would I if I show her the poem?"

Mrs. Johnson sighed. "I can't say whether or not your mother is making a mistake. She is only doing the best she knows." Mrs. Johnson took a deep breath and stared out the window. "In my opinion, she, like I was and maybe still am, is comfortable in her ancient ways and probably will never change." Mrs. Johnson's eyes penetrated Michelette's. "The burden is on you to either accept your mother as she is, and to love her, or to begin a battle that may start building a wall between you. You see, it takes two to build the wall. If you accept her as she is, the wall will not be built. I know that is a lot to ask of a person as young as you, but as I see it, that's the way it is." Mrs. Johnson rose. "Someday, I believe that you'll be able to read the poem to her."

"When?"

"That, dear, is only for you to decide. When that time presents itself, you'll know. It might be today, next week, or next year. But you'll know." Mrs. Johnson hesitated. "And so will she."

Michelette, a gallon plastic bottle of water balanced on her head, and her rainbow backpack dangling from her shoulders, neared the last curve, around which the path leading home would be in sight. Throughout the walk home, she pondered Mrs. Johnson's words. Michelette was pleased that Mrs. Johnson felt her capable of shouldering the responsibility of maintaining the mother/daughter relationship but was uncomfortable accepting such a responsibility. She had to believe that her mother was only doing what she thought right. But in this matter, was there a right and wrong? Knowing that the dilemma was common comforted her, but she was very concerned that she wouldn't have the wisdom to recognize the proper time to show, or not to show, the poem to her mother. Certainly a time like last Friday night wouldn't have been. A thought crossed her mind. Would her mother understand the meaning of the poem? Suddenly she felt ashamed. Of course her mother would.

Just when the path came into sight, so did the familiar United Nations humvee. The vehicle slowed as it approached. All three soldiers smiled and waved.

But this time there was a difference. She didn't like their body language. Maybe they just seemed a little more enthusiastic than usual. Michelette feigned a smile. A knot gripped her stomach. Fear grabbed her breath. The old one riding in front glared at her. The truck rolled on by. She relaxed.

But not for long. The truck stopped. Her stomach crunched so hard it took her breath again. She had heard stories about girls being raped. For the first time in her life, she was scared. Truly scared. Her pace quickened. She glanced back. The truck was turning around! It had never done that before. Before she could get to her path, it pulled alongside and slowed to her brisk pace.

"Want a ride?" the old one asked in broken English. His dark eyes glared at her, and a malicious grin creased his face. A trimmed, heavy black mustache with grey freckles cloaked his lips. Thick eyebrows joined above his big red nose. A wide space between his brown-stained teeth made a light, hissing sound when he breathed. He had a gold emblem on his shoulder.

"No, thank you," Michelette answered nervously, pointing. "I'm almost home. Right up there is the path to my house." She was only steps away, but, with every pace, her trail seemed to drift from her. Her eyes darted between the three men. The driver and the man in back were young. Maybe not much older than she. All three had swarthy complexions. She couldn't identify their nationality but knew they were not African. Her heart raced. Fear gripped her as never before. She had to hide it. She walked faster. Not long to the path. She hoped Eduardo was there.

"That water heavy?" the soldier in back said, also in poor English. "Carry it for you?" He reached for the jug.

Michelette moved out of arm's reach. "No, thank you. It's not heavy." Maybe if she said she appreciated their thoughtfulness, they go away. "I appreciate the offer, though."

"We just want to help," the older man hissed. "Don't you want to get in? We'll take you home." He grinned.

She didn't like the grin.

Finally, she caught up with the path. "This is my path. Bye." She hurried alongside the cane patch and breathed easier as the truck's engine revved. Her pace slowed. She didn't look back, but her heart still pounded.

After several minutes, she relaxed. Then smiled as she heard a familiar rustling of the leaves. Eduardo was about to jump from behind a tree or out of the cane patch.

The old soldier sprang in front of her!

Michelette froze!

"We were trying to help, and you just didn't show any gratitude. Is that a way to treat soldiers trying to bring stability to this godforsaken country?"

Fear shut down her voice. She tried to step off the path and go around, but the man blocked her way. Finally some shaky words came out. "I apologize, sir." She swallowed hard. "I didn't mean to be ungrateful. Please let me go." Tears welled up in her eyes. Her bottom lip trembled

"The girl says she's sorry," the man said, looking over her head. "Should we accept her apology?"

"Let's leave her alone," someone said. "She's only a kid."

"Old enough to bleed, old enough to butcher," the older man said.

He reached out his burly hand and touched Michelette's breast. She shook all over. Bile welled up within. She coughed, and some of the green slime spewed out. The officer cursed and jumped back, but some of her vomit splattered on his pants and shoes. She quickly darted toward the cane patch, dropping the water jug. He grabbed her backpack, jerked her to the ground, and pinned her shoulders. She lay on the pack, her back bowed as if it was going to break.

"Please don't!" she screamed.

"I'm going to give you something good," the old man said, drool hanging from his mustache. "Spit on me, will you!"

Michelette kicked at him, but he pinned her legs with his. She tried to scratch his face. "My mother will know," she yelled. Visions of her mother's friends ravaged by the plague flashed through her mind. Images of sores popping out all over her like they did on her father's sister fueled hysteria. Tears flowed. Stop. She had to control herself. She struggled with all her might. Her mind raced to find an escape.

The man clasped his powerful hand over her mouth and looked at a soldier. "Hold her arms!" The soldier hesitated. "I said hold her goddamn arms. That's an order." He looked at the other. "You hold her legs. The ungrateful little bitch is strong."

Michelette was helpless. There was nothing she could do. She closed her eyes. She didn't want her first time to be like this. His foul body odor penetrated her nostrils. She felt her dress being pulled up. He tugged at her cotton panties, then tore them off. She prayed her mother would believe her. She thought of the last stanza of her poem and repeated it in her mind. "How I react is in my time and space dimension." She would not let this get to her. She felt his weight coming over her. His heavy, smoky garlic breath smothered her face. Her back pressed on the books in her backpack, shooting pain throughout her body. She was better than they. They would not sour her on life. She repeated again in her mind. "How I react is within my own time and space dimension." She tensed and awaited her fate. "In time, this too will pass," she murmured, gritting her teeth.

She heard a dull, forceful thud! "Stop!" yelled Eduardo's familiar voice.

"Ah-h-h-h!" The foul breath over her bellowed in pain.

She opened her eyes as Eduardo, thick tree limb in hand, again hammered the old man, then quickly swung at the other two. They let go. Eduardo yelled into the cane patch. "Marc! Jean-Pierre! Come quick!" He swung and caught the old man across the face. A big, bloody front tooth fell out on Michelette.

"Shoot the bastard!" the man yelled, spitting blood. "Goddamn it, shoot the son of a bitch!"

Michelette leapt to her feet, grabbed Eduardo, and led him as fast as their young legs would go into the cane patch, losing her backpack along the way. The sharp leaves slashed at their arms as they passed through the rows of cane. A shot rang out. Eduardo stumbled, ran through several more rows of cane, then fell to the ground. A pair of heavy black hands reached his armpits, yanked him to his feet, pulled him deeper into the patch, and laid him face down on the ground. The boy was bleeding from a wound in his lower back. The cane worker, machete in hand, signaled for Michelette to lie down and be quiet.

"Don't go in there," a voice rang out. "You can't see a thing!"

"I'm not going to let a couple of fuckin' kids get the best of me," the old man boomed.

Shots rang out. Bullets whizzed over their heads. Eduardo continued to bleed. The worker, with confident eyes and alert hearing, continued to signal for quiet.

A voice from somewhere in the cane patch called in Creole. "Does somebody need help?"

The cane worker put his finger over his mouth. They could hear the soldiers pacing the edge of the patch.

From another direction a Creole voice called, "It came from over there."

They heard distant leaves rustling.

"I'm getting out of here," one of the soldiers said.

"Me, too," said another.

They listened as the soldiers ran. Only as they heard the engine sound die in the distance did they move.

The cane worker stood. "Over here!" he yelled. "Near the road." He turned to Michelette. "We have to get him to the clinic. I have a wagon on the other side. I'll go get it. You wait here."

"We have to tell his mother."

"When someone else comes, you go."

Eduardo lifted his head. "I earned four hundred eighty gourdes today, Michelette." He grimaced, then told her his story.

Michelette started crying. Seeing Eduardo lying bleeding from a gunshot wound was too much.

"Are you happy that I earned the money?"

Michelette realized that Eduardo didn't fully understand the situation. She wiped her nose. "I'm happy for you, Eduardo. Very happy."

"Me, too." He winced again. "What is wrong with me? My back hurts, and I can't move my leg."

"You've been shot." Tears flooded from her eyes. "Shot saving me."

"Did the man hurt you?"

"No. You saved me." Right now she would have been happy to surrender her virginity, even her life, to prevent Eduardo from having to suffer as he was. "Marc is coming with a wagon to take you to the clinic."

"Am I going to Ginen?" Eduardo asked.

"No!"

"Mama tells me that's where Daddy is. If Daddy is there, that must be a good place."

Michelette heard the wagon roll up, and looked up as Marc and two others hacked a path through the cane. They lifted Eduardo and carried him to the two-wheeled cart pulled by a burro. "We'll take him to St. Jude's," Marc said. "They will take him to the clinic."

"I'll go tell his mother. We'll try to catch up."

Michelette ran to Eduardo's house, quickly told his mother, and the two hurried to catch the cart. Jogging all the way, they caught up with the cart just as the entrance to St. Jude's came into view.

Eduardo, in pain, smiled at his mother. "I earned a lot of money today, didn't I, Mama?"

She grabbed his hand and kept pace. "Yes, you did."

Michelette raced ahead to the school. When the cart rolled up, Moland had the truck running. The men lifted Eduardo into the back. His mother and Michelette climbed in with him and sat on the tire well covers, each holding one of Eduardo's hands.

Darkness fell as the truck turned off the main road and headed up the slope leading to the clinic, Moland started blowing the horn. Women and children on the road parted to allow the truck to pass. When he

160

reached the clinic's plateau, he continued to blow the horn while turning and backing to a door. Two men opened the door and stood outside, guiding the truck.

Moland jumped from the truck. "Gunshot wound."

One of the men stuck his head in the door and yelled, "Gunshot victim! Get the doctor."

Blood of Life

Bob, Franck, Presley, and Doctor Pierre Loventure, the clinic's supervising physician, sat in his office enjoying a nightcap when they heard a horn blowing continuously. At first, they didn't think anything about it, but when it continued and got louder, Dr. Loventure rose and walked to the window. The tall doctor carried himself in an elegant, athletic fashion. His smooth bronze complexion belied his forty-five years. He wore a traditional white lab coat with a stethoscope stuffed in its right pocket.

"What is it, Pierre?" Franck asked.

"A truck with two women in the back. Probably bringing somebody in."

"So you're finally going to have to go to work?" Presley asked, smiling.

Dr. Loventure returned the smile. "Not me, smart-ass. I've got good nurses who take care of most of the emergencies. It's probably a woman about to have a baby, and the midwife can handle that better than me." The blasting horn stopped. He returned to his chair and lifted the makeshift tumbler.

Loud and clear the call came. "Doctor. Gunshot wound."

Dr. Loventure leaped to his feet and ran from the room, leaving the stunned men.

"Gunshot wound?" Bob asked.

"Not common here," Presley said. "This is a primary-care clinic, not an emergency room. Unless it's slight, he'll have to send him to Albert Schweitzer on the other side St. Marc, or Foundation Bernard Mevs in Port-au-Prince."

Moments later, Dr. Loventure burst back into the room, snatched the phone off its hook, and dialed. "I've got a gunshot wound here," he said into the phone. "Pretty serious. I can only stabilize him. Can you take him?" He paused. "Are you sure? Best I can tell the boy was shot almost two hours ago. He's lost a bit of blood." Pause. "Okay. Thanks." He placed the phone on the hook. "Shit! We've got to get this kid to Port-au-Prince."

Bob looked at Franck, who said, "We'll take him."

"Great," Dr. Loventure said. "I'll get him ready. At least we can type his blood and call Bernard Mevs to get ready." Dr. Loventure left the room.

"I've got to take the back seat out," Franck said, rising.

"I'll help," Bob said, following Franck.

Outside, as they removed the rear seat from Franck's sport utility, Bob asked, "No ambulance?"

"Only a few in Haiti," Franck said. "Anyway, I've done this before. Let's go inside and see how things are going."

They went into the examination room where the patient lay on a rusting gurney, the doctor busily cleaning the wound. A nurse monitored the patient's blood pressure, and another had an oxygen mask over his face. A frail Haitian woman, doing her best to maintain her composure, stood in the far corner. A young, very pretty Haitian girl sat in a chair, and appeared to be drawing on a sheet of paper.

Bob leaned over to Franck. "That's only a kid."

Franck nodded.

A nurse came in. "Type AB positive," she said. She was American with a distinctive New England accent.

"Do we have any?" Dr. Loventure asked.

"No. Only A."

"That'll have to do," the doctor said. "We have to get some into him or he won't survive the trip."

"I'm AB positive," Bob said.

The doctor turned. "You sure?"

"Yes."

"You want to give some?"

"Yes."

Dr. Loventure stared at him for several moments. "I believe all the equipment is clean, but I can't guarantee it."

"Understood," Bob said. "Let's do it."

"Follow me," the nurse said.

Bob followed the nurse into the next room. She motioned for him to sit in a lounge chair.

"Which arm?" she asked.

"Right."

She set her chair and the equipment next to his right side. "We don't have an autoclave, so we have to boil our equipment and use a disinfectant. It's not as effective as a clave, but we think it's clean."

163

"I'm not particularly worried," Bob said. In fact he was, but a boy's life was worth the risk. He wouldn't have been able to live with himself had he not volunteered.

The nurse sat down, tied a rubber band around his upper arm, and watched as the purple blood vessel in the crook of his arm popped up.

"Good vessel. Looks like you've done this before."

"Many times. How's the boy?"

"Not good." She cleansed his arm with alcohol, then rubbed iodine where she planned to insert the needle. As she finished setting up the bag and tubing, she explained, as she understood, what had happened.

"Shot by a United Nations soldier who was attempting to rape the girl?" Bob said, astonished.

"That's what the girl said. The boy confirmed."

"He's conscious?"

"Yes." Bob felt only a minor prick as she expertly punctured the vessel, taped the needle in place, and made sure the blood flowed easily. "He's a healthy boy, but Doctor Loventure thinks there's internal damage. Maybe a kidney. Internal bleeding is almost guaranteed. If we were a full-fledged emergency room, we probably could save him. Right now, he's fighting bad odds."

"That's too bad," Bob said. "Where are you from and what brings you here?"

"Bangor, Maine. Just came down for a visit, saw a need, and never went back. Except for vacation and to sell my house. Been here two years now. You?"

Bob told her why he was down. He finished as the nurse, blood bag full, disconnected the tubes and taped his arm. "Lie there for a few minutes. I'll be back shortly."

Several minutes later she returned. Bob rose, made sure he wasn't dizzy, then stepped into the examination room to see the blood he had given flowing into the boy's arm.

Dr. Loventure came over and whispered, "If he lives, it'll be your blood that saved his life."

"If?"

"He's in serious condition. When you leave, I'll phone Bernard Mevs and give them advance notice. They'll be ready."

Dr. Loventure checked the boy's vital signs. "Okay, let's get him to the truck. Be careful with the blood."

Two men rolled the boy out while the nurse carried the stainless steel hook holding the blood bag. When they got to Franck's vehicle, she removed the bag from the hook and, holding it above her head, crawled in first, making sure the blood kept flowing. The men cradled the boy and slowly moved him into the truck. Dr. Loventure handed Bob a pillow. As Franck lifted the boy's head and Bob put the pillow in place, the last of the blood flowed into the patient.

The nurse tided up Eduardo's arm, made sure he was as comfortable as possible, and climbed out. The older Haitian woman and the young girl got in, and all slowly started down the bumpy road, women and children parting to let them pass.

The Light

As they turned on to the main road, the man who gave Eduardo blood turned and introduced himself and the driver as Bob Turner and Franck St. Fleur. Michelette introduced herself, Eduardo, and Eduardo's mother.

Eduardo squeezed Michelette's hand. She leaned a little closer. "Is that the man who gave me blood?" Michelette nodded. "Tell him thank you, and that he is a very good man."

"No thanks necessary," Bob said.

Eduardo smiled and opened his eyes wide. He looked around, saw his mother, looked at the back of Franck's head, at Bob, then Michelette, then back at his mother. "Mama?"

"I'm here."

"Mama, today was a good day, wasn't it? I earned a lot of money for us, didn't I, Mama?"

"You sure did, Eduardo. You're a good man."

"Hear that, Michelette? She said I'm a good man. That's the first time she's ever called me a man."

Tears welled up in Michelette's eyes. "You are a good man, Eduardo. A very good man."

"I really gave that soldier a good whop, didn't I?"

"You sure did. A real good one." Michelette started crying.

"Don't cry, Michelette," Eduardo said. "It's been a good day. A day to be happy." Eduardo's eyes turned slowly to his mother. "Daddy will be proud of me, won't he?"

"He would be very proud, son. Very proud." She, too, started crying.

Mr. Turner and Mr. St. Fleur wiped their eyes.

Eduardo looked around. "This is the nicest car I've ever been in." He looked at the light almost directly above him. "Is that a light?"

"Yes," Michelette answered.

Mister St. Fleur must have heard the question because he turned the light on.

"Look, Mama. This car has a light in it." He paused. "Mama?"

"I'm here."

"Mama, I see Daddy. He's smiling. That means he's very pleased with what I did today. He's asking for me to come with him now, Mama."

"No!" his mother said, raising her voice.

"Yes, Mama." Eduardo raised his head toward the light. "Mama, we want you to come be with us."

Eduardo laid his head back on the pillow and went to be with his father.

"Eduardo!" Michelette called. "No!"

Eduardo's mother let out a low, painful wail. Her eyes rolled so high that her dark pupils disappeared. She stopped wailing long enough to catch a breath, screamed as if she had been stuck with a sharp knife, then fainted. She breathed easy. Her face was peaceful. No doubt her ache was so strong that, in defense, her pain center had said enough.

Franck stopped the truck. Together, he and Bob laid the unconscious woman beside her son, raised her feet, and propped them on top of the cooler Franck always carried.

The short journey back to the clinic was silent
except for an occasional deep sob from Michelette,
who had lain down beside her childhood friend and
buried her face in the pillow, raising her head only to
take a breath. Her arm rested on the boy's chest. Just
before they started up the incline to the clinic,
Michelette raised up and looked squarely into
Eduardo's face. "I wish you hadn't come when you
did, Eduardo. It's my fault you're not here anymore."

* * *

Bob didn't know what to say, but he did know the
pain she was going through. The right words would
have been helpful, but he just didn't have them. He
could only reach back and lay his hand on Michelette's
back. Sometimes a touch of human understanding is
enough.

Franck carefully negotiated the vehicle between
mothers and children trickling up the hill. Some carried
bedrolls. Most didn't. On the plateau, the headlights
flashed on women cradling sleeping babies. Children
stopped playing long enough to get out of the way then
resumed after they passed. Around the perimeter,
women had already stretched out for the night, some
on straw mats, some on thin blankets, and some on the
ground. Women outnumbered the men twenty or thirty
to one.

Bob went inside. The staff was cleaning up and
preparing for the next day's onslaught of children
receiving the vaccine. He found Dr. Loventure and
Presley, both of whom were surprised to see him. Bob

explained what had happened. Dr. Loventure, followed by Presley and two Haitian staff members, followed him to the truck where Franck was standing, rear door open. Michelette had sat up, her face buried in her arms. Doctor Loventure removed the cooler and, on his knees, crowded in beside the woman. He took his pencil light from his white lab coat, lifted her eyelid, and flashed a beam into her eyeball. A frown crossed his face. He put the stethoscope in his ears and listened for a heartbeat. Moments later he turned to Bob, Franck, and Presley. "She's dead."

Michelette raised her head and just stared at the doctor. She was probably too numb to feel any more pain. The two staff members mumbled to each other, backed off, then turned and almost ran back into the clinic.

Bob's heart sank. Was there something else he could have done? Had he done the proper thing? What was the girl thinking? How could he possibly make amends? He mentally recounted his steps in checking her. Had he missed something?

Franck patted him on the shoulder. "Don't sweat it, man. There's nothing you could have done to prevent it. It was God's will."

As Doctor Loventure unwound himself from the vehicle, Bob asked, "What do you think happened?"

"The strain was probably too much for her heart, but I can't really say." He looked around. "But I do know we have to get her body out of here, and quick. Rumors about Baron Samedi coming here tonight have probably already started. If we don't get them away immediately, we'll have no one here tomorrow, staff or patients."

"Who's Baron Samedi?" Bob asked.

"Simply put," explained Dr. Loventure, "Baron Samedi is a spirit, or god, that traffics in the souls of the dead. Since the woman died suddenly, some of the staff probably thinks a Loa cast a spell on her and that she was cursed. If they, in any way, attach a curse to this clinic, we've had our last patient and may as well shut down, well and all."

"I agree," Franck said, shutting the rear door. "Come on, Bob. We'll stop out of sight of the clinic."

"I'll follow," Presley said, hurrying to his car.

"What about the girl?" Bob asked.

"We'll get her home," Franck said.

Franck and Bob got back in the truck, and Michelette asked, "Where are we going?"

"We have to get the bodies away from the clinic," Franck explained. "Perhaps we can take them to their family."

"They have no family," Michelette said. "But we can take them home. Mama and I will take care of them."

They drove down the slope in silence. When they hit the main road, Bob turned to Michelette, who was staring at Eduardo. "Excuse me," Bob said, "but if you don't mind, could we ask you about what happened? What caused Eduardo to get shot in the first place? Maybe there's something we can do."

Even the faint glimmer from the truck's dome light didn't hide the vessels in Michelette's teary eyes nor the despairing look on her face. "What does it matter? Eduardo's dead."

Bob sighed and nodded. "Maybe we can prevent it from happening to someone else."

"I can't."

"But maybe I can," Bob countered. "But I'd have to know what happened and, if possible, get a description of the man."

Michelette blankly stared at him, then reached in a pocket in her dress, pulled out several neatly folded sheets of paper, and handed them to him. "Pictures of the men." She tucked up her knees and buried her face in her arms.

Even in the faint light Bob recognized the quality of the sketches. "These are excellent. There should be no problem identifying the men."

When the vehicles rounded the first bend, the clinic out of sight, Franck stopped and explained to Presley what they were going to do. He agreed and left for Port-au-Prince.

An Eye for an Eye

Pearl and Bob Meet Again

As they approached St. Jude's, Michelette said, "If you don't mind, I'd like to stop and tell them what happened."

Franck pulled up by the front gate. Michelette got out, quickly entered the gate, and knocked on Primal Hall's front door. Father Mike answered.

"How's the boy?" he asked. "Moland told me about it."

"He's dead." The reality of her words spread throughout her body. She suddenly grasped the priest, buried her face in his white robe, and cried uncontrollably. He gently wrapped his arms around her shoulders and comforted her. Between sobs, she mumbled, "So is his mother."

Reality wracked her body, and for what seemed like forever, she cried. Several times she thought her legs would collapse. She clung to Father Mike.

Someone else was close. She peered out from her tear-smeared eye. Mr. St. Fleur and Mr. Turner, along with the entire staff of St. Jude, stood nearby. All heads were lowered except Mrs. Johnson's, who looked at her. Michelette let go, wiped her eyes, and went toward her favorite teacher, who met her partway. Receiving comfort only a mother can give, Michelette cried more.

* * *

As Father Mike and Moland went to the truck, Pearl cradled Michelette's head. One of the men, the American, said that the young lady, either in shock or amazing control after what she had been through, had every right to let it all out. He explained to the group what had happened, including that Michelette had enough presence of mind and poise to draw pictures of the men who had attacked her.

Light from Primal Hall was faint, but Pearl thought the American was staring at her. Then she recognized him. Bob Turner! She smiled. His return smile shot the arrow of recognition straight into her heart. She had somewhat settled down from the evening at Moland's, but emotions again pierced her body. She was glad she was holding on to Michelette; but who was supporting whom?

Sister Marie broke the silence. "Well, you two have to have a place to stay. When you take the bodies —"

Michelette's head snapped up. "Eduardo and Marie," she said, wiping her cheek. "Their names were Eduardo and Marie."

"Excuse me. Eduardo's and Marie's bodies home, you'll need a place to stay. We'll have some beds for you. Please come back here for the night."

"Thank you," the Haitian standing next to Bob Turner said. "We'll do that."

Father Mike walked by the group on the way into Primal Hall. "One of them can stay in my room. I'm going to be with Michelette and her mother the rest of the night." He turned to the Haitian. "I'll follow you, if you don't mind." The man nodded.

Natti walked up carrying a basket and handed it to Father Mike. "You need somethin' to feed bodies as well as souls."

"We'll have to make burial arrangements," Moland said.

"I'll discuss that with Michelette's mother," Father Mike said.

* * *

As the school staff went their separate ways, Sister Marie, in a soft voice, called, "Sister Joan, Sister Ester, would you give me a hand making the beds for our guests?"

They both followed Sister Marie into Primal Hall. Sister Marie glanced out the window to make sure that Pearl was out of earshot, then turned to the two nuns. "I don't think this will have an effect on Pearl's anniversary party unless the memorial for her friends is at a time when Michelette can't come, do you?"

Each shook their head, but Sister Joan, smiling as always, suggested, "We could offer the use of the Shelter for the memorial Friday night. That way everything would be over by Saturday night, so everyone could still come."

"I'm not so sure about that," Sister Ester said. "Haitian funerals can go for a long time. Depending on how many come and how much tafia they drink, the party, service, or whatever it evolves into may go on until the wee hours."

"Sister Joan may have a point, though," Sister Marie said. "By that time, the mourning period will be over, and partying, if it is still going on, will be in full swing. We were concerned about how we were going to be able to decorate the Shelter without Pearl becoming suspicious. She would also be suspect when people began showing up. This way, with a lot going on, she might not get any clues and could even help. I'll talk to Father Mike in the morning. What about her son and daughter?" the elder sister asked.

Unknown to Pearl, the sisters, along with Father Mike and Moland, had scrimped and saved a portion of the funds necessary for Beverly and Wayne to fly in, and Wayne, touched by their gesture, agreed to pay the remainder. Francois and Georges were to pick them up at the airport in Port-au-Prince on Friday and take them to her place where they would spend the night, then the staff was going to shift sleeping arrangements so the family could stay together at St. Jude's. The two had reservations to fly back on Tuesday.

"Everything is set," Sister Joan said. "We received final confirmations yesterday, and Francois is ready for them."

"And how's the gift coming?" Sister Marie asked.

"It's finished," Sister Ester answered, raising her eyebrows. "Whose idea was that terrible thing anyway?"

"Ester!" Sister Marie said. "Don't you dare say such a thing in front of anyone else."

"I won't, but that thing scares me to death when I look at it."

Sister Joan squealed with joyous anticipation. "Is it here?"

Sister Ester did the holy cross. "Mercy, no. I'll not bring that hideous thing into Primal Hall!" Her hands punctuated the air. "It's still over at that artist's house, and as far as I'm concerned, that's where it can stay. I don't know what got into Father Mike, telling those girls to make something that could be interpreted as Haitian theology!"

"Now, Ester," Sister Marie said.

"Have you seen that hideous thing?" Sister Ester asked.

"Yes."

"And you approve?"

"Well," she said, "it is appropriate."

Sister Ester again did the holy cross. "Lord, Mother of God, please watch over us."

Sister Joan choked back laughter.

The Shadows

Silence reigned as Franck, following Michelette's precise instructions, led the two-vehicle procession to her path, where they turned off and carefully bumped along beside the cane field, dodging trees and bushes. Bob's mind was back at the school. Several times he had turned and looked at Michelette. She was a pretty, intelligent, innocent girl who had just been through a horrifying encounter that no being should experience. Perhaps he was just feeling empathic.

He again turned and looked at her. She was cradling Eduardo's head, and steadying his mother's so it wouldn't bounce off the rolled-up sleeping bag Franck kept. But she hung in.

Suddenly, she stiffened. "There," she said, pointing. "Over there. Edge of the light. Our water bottle." She looked around. "There! Right there. That's where it happened."

"Want to take a look?" Franck asked.

Michelette thought for a minute. "I'd like to find my backpack."

Bob opened the door. "I'll get the water bottle."

Franck reached behind and under his seat, and handed Bob a four-cell flashlight. "Here's a lantern. Watch your step. I'll pull around so my headlights flood the area."

Bob explained to Father Mike what was happening, picked up the water, and walked toward where the vehicles had pulled alongside. He watched as Franck, Father Mike, and Michelette crawled from the vehicles. The men walked into the lighted area while Michelette disappeared into the cane. As he approached, the flashlight's beam caught something. He picked up what appeared to be an epaulet from a soldier's uniform.

Michelette, backpack in hand, emerged from the cane field. "I think I remember something falling out of the man's mouth when Eduardo hit him. It would be right in here somewhere." Suddenly, she plopped down, covered her face with her hands, and started wailing. Father Mike laid his hand on her shoulder.

Several shadows emerged from the cane patch, all carrying machetes in the ready position. "Franck," Bob whispered and nodded. "Over there."

Franck looked, then spoke rapidly in Creole. Father Mike and Michelette raised their heads.

"Jean-Pierre?" Michelette said. "Marc?"

"Mikey," came a Creole accented voice from the shadows. "You okay?" More shadows emerged from the patch.

Michelette stood. "Yes, but Eduardo and his mother are in Ginen with his daddy."

As one, the shadows approached, lowering their machetes. Michelette explained the day's events while Franck picked up something and handed it to Bob, who examined it. Bob showed the group the epaulet. "With this, and Michelette's sketches, I'll go to the United Nations. Should not be difficult pinpointing responsibility."

The shadows mumbled and shifted. Bob did not get a happy feeling. Their talk grew louder. One glared at Bob and spoke sharply to the shadow called Marc. Several others appeared to be working themselves into frenzy. Franck spoke in Creole. From gestures, Bob knew Franck had asked a question. The shadows settled down a bit as the man Michelette referred to as Jean-Pierre delivered a short, animated speech while Franck intently listened. When Jean-Pierre stopped, Franck turned to Bob.

"They insist that you do not go to the United Nations."

"Why not? We have sufficient proof. Surely these guys have to be punished!"

"This is far from the first time this has happened here in Haiti," Franck explained. "Outsiders have been raping our women for a long time. It's common knowledge that the United Nations soldiers stick together. At the first sign of trouble, the problem soldiers go home and the ones who stay get really mean, especially to those suspected of causing trouble. They," he said, referring to the shadows, "prefer to handle the situation themselves."

Bob's eyes scanned the group. For the first time, he actually counted them. Twenty or so men and three women. All with serious eyes. "Oh!" Bob said. "And have they?"

The shadows stirred again.

"You should not ask that," Franck said.

"O-o-okay," Bob replied. "I didn't ask, and will not ask again." To prove his sincerity, he threw the epaulet and tooth into the cane patch and brushed his hands together, showing that he was cleaning his hands of the situation. Flashing white smiles dotted the shadows, but the eyes stayed serious. Bob breathed a sigh of relief.

"Let's go on home," Michelette said. This time, she did not ride. She melted in with the shadows.

As the vehicles crawled into the night, the shadows followed. A single, gentle female voice laced with emotion chanted mournfully. After several verses, more voices joined in and shared the pain. As the procession moved along, additional shadows from both sides of the path joined the mourners. A torch sprang to light, and from the one came many. The torchbearers and agonizing chant depicted the day's tragedy more beautifully than any chorus in any opera Bob had ever heard.

* * *

Franck and Bob made their way back toward the main road. One of the shadows rode on the hood, guiding them. "Well, if you had to guess, what do you think will happen to the UN fellows?"

Franck watched the guide carefully. "You don't really want to know, and I don't know for sure. But, if I had to guess, I would say that boiling pots somewhere nearby have three very big pieces of meat and lots of bones in them, and, from the stainless steel coils topping each will come a special liquid. The drink will be used in a ritual when the solids from the kettles, less bones, of course, are buried. The bones will be used in special ceremonies." The shadow on the hood motioned for Franck to jog left. He did. "I would also guess that the clothing was part of the fire."

"Will we ever know?"

"No, but if you want some secondary proof of my theory, listen for drums tonight or tomorrow night."

"I hear drums almost every night when in the countryside."

"These will be different. You'll know."

"How about the vehicle, equipment, and weapons?"

"The equipment will either be used or sold on the black market, or both. The guns and ammunition will be sold. The vehicle, on the other hand, is probably deep in the woods under thatch. The markings will be taken off and serial numbers destroyed. It will be repainted, then stored and well-taken care of until it can safely be moved upcountry and used on some plantation. Plantation owners are the only ones that would want a vehicle like that."

"So you think the matter has already been settled."

"Yes."

"Swift justice."

"Haitian justice."

"What now?"

"United Nations Police will come looking and asking questions. Nobody will say anything. Rumors will start and conveniently find their way into the United Nations compound. Things will settle down, then a new wave of troops will come in. Then we'll have a dozen or so more rapes, and somewhere, sometime the UN will receive the same education with the same results."

"Seems kinda uncivilized."

"No more uncivilized than rape," Franck replied. "Besides, is it any more humane to keep them caged like animals the rest of their lives?"

Bob's Concern

As they reached the road, the shadow jumped off, waved, and disappeared into the night. Bob tilted the seat back, removed his shoes, and propped one foot on the dash. "Boy, what a day!"

"You owe me a bunch for that experience. That's not in your average tourist brochure."

"Boy, I'll say."

"I saw you looking at that teacher at St. Jude's. Was she the one in Pétionville?"

"Yes. Nice lady."

"That's all you can say?"

"Yep." And that was all he was going to mention on the subject, mainly because he really didn't know what to say. An empty sensation shrank his stomach as he recalled Pearl comforting Michelette. He was recalling Sarah comforting one of the kids. Sarah's image was blurred. Bob, trying to bring her back into focus, closed his eyes tight and pressed his fingers against his forehead.

"Got a headache?"

"Nope. Just tired, I guess. It's after midnight. I'll be glad to get to bed. Any bed."

"Any bed?"

"I'm too tired to even think of that."

But was he really? For the first time since his wife had died, he felt a longing for the compassionate, uncompromising touch of an understanding female. He didn't want to admit it, but his scrotum felt like it was filled with lead, the only time since Sarah had become sexually incapacitated, many months before her death.

"Bed just ahead," Franck said as St. Jude's came into view.

As they approached, Bob noticed one of the sisters in a chair just inside the gate, her chin resting on her chest. When the full force of the headlights landed, her head snapped up. She rose and opened the gate.

Franck rolled down the window.

"Please park right over there," Sister Joan said, pointing. "I'll show you to your rooms."

After a quick tour of Primal Hall and explanation of the morning routine, Bob pulled off his shoes and stretched out across the bed, hoping for sleep to come quick. It didn't. Even the pleasant sounds of crickets didn't lull him to sleep. He watched the ceiling fan turn. He tried to count its revolutions. It didn't work. He tried counting just one blade as it crossed a crack in the ceiling. That didn't work either.

Then he thought he heard drums. Eerily, the crickets stopped. Only the ceiling fan swooshed. Bob turned it off and listened. Faint, but they were there. As he listened, the beats seemed to create the stillness of the night. These were not the typical happy dance drums. He got out of bed and stood by the open window.

A cloud loomed overhead and plunged the area into lunar darkness. A breeze guided drumbeats across the water. The long moan of a musician's horn penetrated the night. The wind blew harder, and the sad wails of music haunted the air. His heart pumped to the rhythm; his breathing felt like the gusting wind. A bolt of lightning, followed by earsplitting thunder, struck a nearby tree. The drums did not miss a beat.

Two smaller bolts thundered across the sky. The ghoulish rhythm possessed the night.

He watched the tree smolder and listened as the stirring wind carried the message to understanding ears.

Justice had been served.

Bob had scarcely dropped off when the *whomp, whomp, whomp* announcing breakfast jarred him awake. He quickly rinsed his unshaven face, straightened his clothing as best as he could, and made his way into the dining room, where Moland and Sisters Marie and Ester were already seated. Sister Marie motioned for him to sit next to her. As he took his chair, he observed that the lazy susan in the center of the table had fresh orange juice, milk, water, coffee, a plate of fresh mango slices, a basket of homemade raisin muffins, and a cup of sugar. Franck came in and, following Sister Marie's silent instruction, took a seat next to Sister Ester. An outside door opened and Sister Joan walked in, followed by Pearl. A tingling sensation trailed down Bob's spine. Sister Joan quickly took her normal chair, which was next to Franck's. The only seat left, other than Father Mike's, was next to Bob. Pearl came over. Instinctively, and nervously, Bob rose and assisted with her chair. He glanced around. Everyone was looking at them. Their arms brushed, triggering a forgotten sensation.

As he sat down, he leaned over to Pearl and whispered, "Did I make a social miscue?"

"No miscue," Pearl answered quietly, "just not a courtesy to which we're accustomed."

"Good."

"If you two Americans are finished talking," Sister Marie said, "we'll say grace."

"We're finished," Bob and Pearl said in unison.

A humorous murmur followed, as did Sister Joan's blessing, which included a silent moment for the two deceased, and thanks for the visitors.

After Natti took orders, Sister Ester spoke. "What an eerie night!"

"Those drums penetrated my very soul," said Sister Joan, munching on her second muffin.

"I came straight out of bed when that lightening hit," Pearl said. Holding the coffee, she offered to pour some for Bob.

"Yes, thank you." Bob noticed her hand trembled, probably from the weight of the coffeepot. "Here, let me." He reached to help her, and she spilled a little into his saucer.

"I'm sorry," she said.

"My fault," he replied. "I should have let you finish." His stomach was so nervous he wasn't sure he could eat. Why was he feeling this way? "Anyway, I was standing in the window and saw the lightening bolt hit a tree somewhere over that way." He nodded his head. "It was close." He sipped his coffee.

"Cream or sugar?" Pearl asked.

"No, thanks," Bob's heart thumped.

"But what about those drums?" Sister Marie asked, looking straight at Moland, who had not spoken.

"Those drums," he said in his ministerial voice, "were the drums of the cycle of life."

"The cycle of life?" Pearl asked.

"Yes." The old man's eyes met all those at the table before he spoke again. Bob felt a sudden chill when Moland's eyes met his. "This time," Moland said, "they spoke of death."

"Of course," Sister Ester said. "They were mourning the death of the boy and his mother."

Everyone but Moland and Franck, the only Haitians, continued preparing coffee and munching. Imperceptive to the others, the countrymen nodded. Then Franck glanced at Bob. The communication was clear. Say no more about the drums.

Sister Joan taste tested everything on the rotating center, some twice, and encouraged Franck to try everything as well.

Pearl offered Bob a muffin, which he accepted.

"Thank you," he said, taking a small bite. That was all his stomach could handle. "Say, this is pretty good."

"Natti's a great cook," Pearl replied. "I've really put on weight since I've been here."

"Then you must have been very skinny when you came," Bob said.

Pearl felt herself blush. "Why, thank you."

"Mr. Turner," Sister Marie said, "would you happen to be the same man who said something to Mrs. Johnson, er, Pearl, about possibly getting us some computers?"

"Computers?" piped in Sister Ester. "When and what kind? Do we have a choice? How about a good Internet connection and a printer and a scanner and a router?"

"Slow down," Sister Marie said. "Don't scare him off."

"Yes," Bob said, looking at Pearl. "I believe I can get some. It would help if I had a list, which," he looked at Sister Ester, "I believe should be no trouble."

"No trouble at all," Sister Ester said, reaching for a pad of paper and a pencil.

Natti entered, and everyone chatted as the food was set in front of them.

"I really enjoyed the dance last weekend," Pearl said. "I'm not really sure I thanked you enough. But, I might say, I was very surprised to see you last night. How did you get involved?"

Bob briefly explained the clinic and everything that had happened, leaving out Franck's theory on the drums. "We hadn't planned on spending the night. All my stuff is still back at the Creole." He placed his utensils on his plate, indicating that he was finished, and brushed his facial stubble. "Couldn't shave or change clothes. But enough about me. You must really like it here."

"I do," Pearl said, picking at her still-uneaten egg. "Life is simple and easy. Just what I needed at this time in my life." She took one bite of her toast.

Bob sensed an epiphany coming. "And what time is that?"

Before Pearl could answer, Sister Marie interrupted. "Well, is there anything going on today that I should know about?"

"I'm getting a high-tech list together," Sister Ester said, with an impish smile and gleam in her eyes. She

187

rattled off everything on her list. "Did I miss anything?"

"How about a water pump," Moland asked. Everyone chuckled

"Never ask, never receive, we always say," Sister Ester said. "There you are, Mr. Turner."

"That was quick," Bob said, glancing over the list, then folding and putting it in his pocket. He felt as if he had known everyone in the room for years. He was comfortable. Almost.

From the commotion outside, it became apparent that the students were arriving. The sisters, as if on cue, rose simultaneously. Pearl started to get up. Bob began to rise to help, but Pearl put her hand on his arm as a reminder, and Bob remained seated. As she pushed away, she asked, "When will you be going back?"

"Probably within the hour."

"It was nice seeing you again."

"Thanks. For me, too."

Everyone but Moland, Franck, and Bob left. Natti came in with a cup of coffee and sat. As Moland started to speak, Father Mike walked in carrying the basket, set it against the wall, and took a seat.

"Had breakfast?" Natti asked.

"No. How about some bananas and toast?"

"Yes, sir." Natti rose. "Melon?"

"Please." Natti disappeared through the door. "What a night! There must have been a hundred or more coming by to honor the dead. And those drums. I haven't slept a wink."

"How's the girl?" Bob asked.

"She's fine. Naturally, she won't be at school today. Probably not tomorrow. Her mother seems okay, but she looks really frail. It's been a long time since I've seen her but I think something's wrong. We ought to get her in for an exam."

Sister Marie came back in. "How's Michelette?"

Father Mike explained again.

"We were thinking last night that if we offer the Shelter for a service Friday night, then that would help solve several problems in decorating for Pearl's party Saturday night." She explained the final plans, and Father Mike gave his approval.

"Pardon me for being nosy," Bob asked, surprising himself, "But I'm interested in this party Saturday night."

Sister Marie told him about the party, including Pearl's children coming in.

"Would it take away from the party if we could get the computers here by then?"

"Oh, no," Father Mike exclaimed. "It would enhance the celebration."

"Mr. Turner," Moland said.

"Please call me Bob."

Moland nodded. "Bob, perhaps you could bring the computers?"

Bob looked at Franck.

"I can't come," Franck said, "but you could use the Ford. I don't need it until Monday. I could pick it up at the Creole Sunday night." He rose. "We better hit the road."

Bob rubbed his head. "I'll see what I can do." He took a final sip of coffee, rose, said thanks, and followed Franck out.

As they drove from the compound, Franck said, "A member of our Rotary Club, Ben Alce, is the largest computer dealer in Port-au-Prince. Maybe he could help."

"We'll have to price this out, but it could be up to ten thousand dollars, U.S. Could be tough to come up with that much by Saturday."

On their way to the Creole, they stopped by Ben's place and explained the situation.

Ben said all equipment but the scanner and router was in stock. He priced out the bill of materials. Bob glanced at the total. "Oh, what the hell." He reached in his pocket, pulled out his billfold, and handed Ben his credit card. "I'll get our club to pay for most of it. I need to pick the stuff up Saturday morning."

* * *

Franck's home, about twenty minutes from the hotel, sat high on one of the hillsides overlooking the southern part of Port-au-Prince. As Franck punched the button opening the security gate, he asked, "Come in for a refresher?"

"Why not?" Bob answered. "Only an empty room waiting back at the Creole."

Franck knew from the response that Bob was in one of his ever more frequent down moods. "Sorry we didn't have room for you to stay with us this time."

"Oh, I didn't mean to imply anything." Bob opened the door as Monique, Franck's lovely wife, came from of the house.

"Bob!" Monique exclaimed, giving him a big hug. "I was wondering if you were going to come up and see me this trip. Stay for dinner?"

"I'd like to," Bob answered, "but it's been a rough week." He paused. "But I could use one of your special punches."

"Great. I have some in the fridge. I'll bring it up to the patio. Franck?"

"A beer. Do we have any snacks?"

"Kids are hitting the pantry pretty hard, but I think I might have something." She disappeared into the house.

Through hard work and created opportunities, Franck and Monique had joined the upper middle class in Haiti. His first wife, from the real upper class, wanted Franck to take what her family chose to give, which, of course, came at a price that Franck, ultimately, was not willing to pay. He readily admitted that all the signals were there, but being only nineteen, rampaging hormones interfered with good judgment. The childless marriage had lasted barely a year. He always admitted, in private, of course, that the sex was nothing short of great, but the price was just too high.

He had met Monique two years after the divorce. She was studying to be a doctor, a personally rewarding but financially depressed profession in Haiti. Together they had built what they now had; a beautiful, debt-free home, and three grown children, two of whom were newlyweds. All lived in the same

191

compound because none of the children, all college graduates, could afford to live elsewhere.

Monique joined Franck and Bob on the rooftop patio. A gray haze covered Port-au-Prince. She handed Franck his beer and a frosted glass, set two glasses of ice, a pitcher of golden rum punch, and a bowl of roasted peanuts in the middle of the glass-topped table. Bob filled Monique's glass, then his. She stuck a reusable reed straw in each and sat down.

"I feel kinda bad, keeping you from your family," Bob said, taking a long draw from his punch.

"No problem," Franck said, looking at his friend. "So you're feeling lonely?"

"That's not the word for it." Bob took another draw.

Franck held up the mug. "It's been an unusual few days."

"Tell me about it," Monique asked, looking at Bob.

For the next several minutes, Franck and Bob explained the happenings of the past several days, taking time to elaborate in minute detail every time Monique asked one of her frequent questions. As they talked, the sun dropped into the Caribbean Sea, and the lights in some sections of Haiti's capital city came on.

As Bob explained about the computers, the compound's generator started. Franck listened intently as it searched for its proper operating output. When it began purring like a large house cat, he relaxed.

When Bob finished talking, he took another long draw, then set his glass down. Two lighted sections of Port-au-Prince darkened while the street lights in two dark sections came on. "I see they still don't have full power output."

"Been four months of rotating blackouts," Franck said, "and will probably be three or four more until the transformer is shipped in and replaced, and the two oil generators are repaired."

"So, are you dating anyone?" Monique asked, quickly bringing the subject back to Bob. "You mentioned lonely was not the word for the way you apparently feel, so I assume you've got someone back in the States."

Bob smiled wryly. "No one."

"Still grieving Sarah?" Monique asked.

"I guess." He took another drink. "I think I've been hitting this stuff a bit hard recently." He refilled his glass. "It helps relieve the darkness."

"So I noticed." Franck sipped his beer. "I was lonely right after my divorce."

"You weren't lonely," Monique joked. "You were sexually deprived."

Bob chuckled, then fell serious. "Maybe one happy marriage is all I should expect." His eyes glistened.

"That's not true," Franck said, scooping several peanuts from the dish.

"Happiness is what you make it," Monique said. "I suspect you and Sarah supported each other's strong points, and complemented each other's weaknesses. Kinda like those Rotary gears you and Franck are always talking about." She joined the fingers of both hands imitating interlocked gears. "You meshed well together, and that takes two. Since you found it once, if

193

you gather your courage and open yourself to opportunity, you'll find it again."

Franck emptied his mug.

"Want another?" Monique asked.

"I think so."

Monique rose and disappeared into the house. The men sat silently watching the lights in other sections of the city rotate off and on.

"I hope she's right," Bob finally said, drawing down the punch.

"She usually is. You're a considerate person. Look what you have just done. Given blood to a dying boy under fairly risky conditions. Buying computers for a school of which you have absolutely no history. Taking the lead on getting a generator for a clinic in need. Happiness isn't going to come to you. You have to be open to it." He paused. "And you can be, but not through that." He tapped on the pitcher.

"But it helps me through the low spots," he took a small sip, "which have been coming more frequently and getting longer."

Monique returned and handed Franck an open, frost-covered beer, refilled the bowl of peanuts, and sat.

"Bob, it's really none of my business, and I don't want to sound like a preacher," Franck said, "but you must remember that no one can replace Sarah. Besides, it wouldn't be fair of you to expect anyone to." He paused. "My guess is that Sarah loved you enough that she would not have wanted you to go through rest of your life alone."

"But I have the kids."

"But they, as they should, have their own lives to live. You should not depend on them to fill the void Sarah left in your heart because they can't do it." Franck was concerned that he was being too harsh with his good friend, but knew of no other way. He felt that their friendship was strong enough to survive a little blip, should this be one.

"A friend of mine," Monique interjected, obviously sensing Franck's concern, "lost her husband of fifteen years recently in an automobile accident. As he took his last breaths, he said to her, 'I hope you miss me, but you have to let me go. With all my love, I leave you.'" Monique rested her hand on Bob's. "Perhaps you should miss her, but let her go."

* * *

Bob drove Franck's sport utility back to the Creole. He paused overlooking the bar, thought about a nightcap, then reluctantly went to his room. Again he tossed and turned, and was awake when first light filtered through the bougainvillea shading the window. A hummingbird hovered in front of a maroon blossom, then, like a kid facing a dessert buffet, darted from one to another. "Miss her but let her go" echoed in the canyons of his mind. He missed Sarah, but had not let her go.

How could he?

The Memorial Service

Father Mike's Counsel

After class, Pearl walked toward Primal Hall, hoping to con Natti out of some lemonade. It had been a strange week. First, the past weekend had been emotionally unsettling, more so because she couldn't pinpoint the reason, or reasons, for her internal upheaval. Then came the session at Moland's, and Francois's little dissertation on the five levels of love, concepts she was still having difficulty understanding, much less accepting. Then the night at the beach. Had the entire evening been a dream, or had it really happened? Who was the couple? Where had they gone? And just when her emotions were taking refuge behind rational thought, she again came face-to-face with Bob Turner. The turmoil started anew, fueled by the drums of life. And at breakfast this morning, with Bob sitting beside her, she was so flustered she couldn't eat and so klutzy she almost spilled coffee all over him and herself. Now she was drained from trying to stay focused all day in class. Her tongue felt like cotton. She was hungry, but her squeamish stomach said to be careful.

She walked by Moland, who was preparing a door of the Louvre for a fresh coat of paint. "He's the one, isn't he?" The voice was so soft and indirect that she almost thought the words came from her subconscious. Pearl stopped and looked at the smiling old man.

"What are you talking about?" she asked.

Moland kept smiling, a mischievous sparkle in his eye. "You know."

Pearl shifted from one foot to the other. "No, I don't."

"Then why did you stop?"

Like a guilty child, Pearl glanced around to make sure no one was listening. "Is anyone in there?" She nodded toward the toilet. Moland shook his head. "How did you know? Was it the way I acted at breakfast?"

Moland smiled.

"Moland," Pearl said, as if chastising one of her students. "Don't just stand there grinning. Say something! Did I make a fool of myself this morning?"

"No, but from the way I saw things, I think you should be ready to see Mr. Turner again, and in the not too distant future."

Pearl's heart leapt. "Is he coming back?"

"I'd say within the next two or three days."

"To bring the computers?"

"No, to see you."

Pearl stared at the old man. She could feel tears welling up in her eyes. "Please don't play with me, Moland. I don't think I can handle it right now."

Moland laid down the scraper and put his hand on her shoulder. "I'm not playing, Pearl. I saw something between you. He'll be back."

"Oh, Lord, what am I going to do? I can't take much more of this. Last week, life was so simple." She brushed away a tear. "And at my age, I feel so foolish."

"I don't know what you're gonna do," he said, picking a red double hibiscus in full bloom from a nearby bush, "but I do know that life, in all its glory, is to be lived, not endured." He tucked the flower over her right ear.

Pearl stared at Moland's wise face. His words struck home. In silence, she embraced the old man, turned, and walked to Primal Hall. This time, she was not going to the dining room. She was going into its small chapel. She decided that it was necessary to talk with Father Mike, not as a teacher at his school, but as a Catholic and member of his parish.

Waiting for the priest, Pearl knelt at the railing and stared up at the brass crucifix on the altar. Her arms rested on the banister, her entwined fingers cradling the red blossom. "Mother of God, what am I to do? My daughter has virtually disowned me. The Church says there are things that I must do and things I must not do. I have tried to be a good person and do everything right. I think I have obeyed all the rules, but I'm miserable. My heart is screaming for something, and I don't know what. I just don't know what to do."

She heard the door open and waited in silence as Father Mike approached and knelt beside her. In his priestly voice, he asked, "What is it, Pearl?"

Tears streamed down her cheeks. "I have tried to be a good Catholic, Father. Really tried. I have always

attended mass. I went to confession when I had
nothing to confess. I have always believed in God. I
have never lain with a man other than my husband. I
raised two children, although neither is a devout
Catholic. Now a voice inside me is saying that
something is wrong. I'm having yearnings that could
be called sinful. If my heart is in the right place, as it
should be because I've been obedient, why should I be
feeling so empty inside, and so guilty? Is it possible
that, in all my years, I have been wrong? Tell me,
Father, have I been wrong?"

"No, you have not been wrong."

"Then why am I in such agony?"

"I cannot say. Perhaps you can tell me more about
your pain. Perhaps together we can make something of
it."

Pearl had, at the beginning of her tenure at St.
Jude's, told Father Mike all the facts about her
marriage with Ted, including his infidelities and his
striking her, and about the conflict with her daughter.
This time, she repeated everything, but with emotion.
Just before she finished, she added, "But I'm terribly
lonely, and feel like I have been all my life. I didn't
know it until last weekend. Then watching Francois
and Georges dance . . . then you and I talked
afterward."

"And Mr. Turner came into your life again."

Pearl sighed, turned, and sat on the kneeling
cushion, leaning back against the railing. "Does
everybody know about Mr. Turner and my life?"

Father Mike turned and sat beside her. "I don't think so. But perhaps you are in turmoil because you have something to confess."

Pearl shrugged her shoulders. "Hardly, but if I keep seeing him, I can't be so sure, and maybe that's what's troubling me, but you, being a priest, probably wouldn't understand."

Father Mike looked up at the ceiling. "Oh, I see. My oath of celibacy. Well, let me tell you that it's the spirit of love that makes celibacy easy for me. My love of God, and my love for all my parishioners. Without that love, I couldn't do it."

Pearl tried to gather her thoughts. "So if I loved God and all my students, I wouldn't be going through all this pain?"

"I didn't say that. All I said was that love is what works. Remember Francois's five levels?"

"Somewhat," she said, bordering on lying. They had been rolling over and over in her mind, but she kept getting them confused.

Father Mike briefly reviewed the first three levels, then said that the fourth was the true love that two people have for each other and that the fifth level was the love that transcends all logic and society's mores, the type of love that priests try to attain as affirmed by, among other things, celibacy. "But before we go any further on that, do you think you truly love your husband?"

Pearl twirled the red hibiscus, looked up at the cracked ceiling, then at the small mahogany cross on the chapel wall. She felt inexplicably comfortable with him, a priest, sitting beside her, at her level, not hidden behind a screen. Strangely, she felt as if he was treating her as an equal. Even though he was about her son's age, she was more comfortable with him than she ever had been with any other man of the cloth. "I don't know, Father. I never felt bells ringing or anything like that around him. We just seemed to evolve."

"Do you miss him now? Did you cry when you split?"

"No to both," she answered quickly, still twirling the flower. "As a matter of fact, just the opposite. When he moved out, I was relieved, but I still feel somewhat guilty about that. Like it was my fault. Even so, I can't think of any circumstance where I would go back."

"Perhaps you are attempting to finally achieve a level of love higher than that of your animal nature. Perhaps your heart is telling you that you must go into the next level, but your brain is resisting."

"But I can't go back to Ted! That's not what my heart is saying."

"Mr. Turner?"

"But I can't commit adultery, can I?"

"I can't tell you what you can and cannot do. But I can tell you that all have sinned and fallen short of the glory of God, and that God will forgive your sins."

"So I can go on living like I am, or I have to become an even greater sinner and hope for forgiveness."

"Or find in yourself God's will. Only then will you find true happiness."

"What if it means divorce and remarriage?"

"Remember the fifth level of love, the level that transcends society's mores."

"What if it means adultery?"

"Remember the fifth level of love."

Pearl hesitated. She nervously fingered the beautiful flower, but had to ask the next question. "What if it means suicide?"

"Remember the fifth level of love, the love that breaks into the transcendent. It surpasses all else, including self and society."

"If I got a divorce, could I stay here and teach?"

"On behalf of the Church, I can't sanction divorce."

That answer cut Pearl to the core. She recalled the Sisters back in Tampa. Follow the rules of the Church! Sex was only for procreation! Endure the marriage! Now gentle, understanding Father Mike was laying down the rule. Then she reviewed silently love's various levels. The rules levels. Levels one and two. She was not a child. She was beyond these levels. But where? A tempest stirred within. More damn rules! She almost crushed the blossom.

In a calming voice, Father Mike spoke. "Living in the spirit demands going beyond the rational. Each of us has a spirit and a brain. The rational of the brain is conditioned by the culture in which we find ourselves. Our spirits are eternal. To find spiritual truth, one must transcend the rational programming of society." He paused. "All of society."

Pearl knew he was trying to give her some insight, but something, perhaps her anger, blocked him out.

She started to rise. "I'm sorry, Father. You're beyond me."

He rested his hand on her arm. "Please?"

She looked into his eyes, saw a compassionate spirit, and relaxed.

"The transcendental voyage from the rational to the spiritual is like taking a one-way trip —"

"A one-way trip?"

"It's one way, because once you go beyond the rational into the spiritual, you can never go back. But that's not the point of my story."

"I'm sorry?"

"No problem." He drew two imaginary circles on the dust-free floor. "Let's imagine that the name of this," he said, pointing to one circle, "is Rational Island, and this one," he said, pointing to the other, "is Spiritual Island. You're going to take a sailboat from one to the other, across the turbulent waters of life."

"Okay," Pearl said, wondering where this little story was going.

"You get into the boat, sail across, get out, and experience the ecstasy of Spiritual Island. You know that you will never go back to Rational Island. As you explore and experience the beauty of Spiritual Island, do you pick up the sailboat and carry it with you, or do you leave it behind?"

"You leave it behind, of course."

"Do you love and respect the boat because it carried you across the treacherous waters?"

"Yes."

"Do you stay beside the boat and worship it because of what it did for you?"

"No."

Father Mike just looked at her.

The analogy began to make sense.

"The same is true of whatever vehicle takes you from the rational into the spiritual world," the priest said. "Now let me make a confession. The Catholic Church, with all its man-made failings, was my sailboat. It is the vehicle upon which I arrived, as a teenager, right here in Haiti. And I find it rather easy to practice the priesthood, including celibacy. Humbly speaking, I believe I am living in the spirit. I am not overly obsessed with the rules that kept the boat afloat, and I can see the many other vehicles traveling the spiritual route, including voodoo. However, as a priest, I sometimes think myself a rudder, and the Church the boat, trying to guide people on their journey to Spiritual Island. Often, I feel very inadequate, as I do right now. I sense that you, for much of your life, have been sailing into the wind, that the Church has so rusted your rudder with rules that you have not been allowed to adjust your course, to tack into the wind. I sense that your uneasiness lies in the fact that you now see your destiny, but because the rudder is stuck in place, you can't get there."

"How can we free the rudder?"

"We can't. You're the boatman, Pearl. Only you can free the rudder."

For the moment, his demeanor of treating her as an equal, and his little story, washed away her anger and tension. She felt she was on the verge of understanding what was going on in her mind.

"Only you can clean away the rust." He paused. "And, as on a real boat, keeping ahead of corrosion is a never-ending task, particularly the extreme, but subtle, effect of social duties." He paused again. "Social duties can have a devastating effect on one's spiritual life."

Pearl felt a flake of rust fall from the rudder of her conscience. Some of what Father Mike had said was the same thing Beverly had been saying, though definitely not in the same words. Perhaps the first true step in taking control of her own providence was, if she could find the correct words, to sit down and write Bev. She would make a point this weekend to take pencil and paper out to the beach.

"How do you feel?" Father Mike asked.

Pearl leaned over, pecked him on the cheek, and gave him a hug. "Thank you."

She had never before kissed or hugged a priest.

Jim Henry

Preparations for the Memorial Service

Pearl found the Shelter busy with somber activity. A boom box played African chants and instrumental music. Michelette, her body keeping time with the music, taped a posterboard-sized charcoal of Eduardo, sitting on a tree limb, on the Shelter's only wall. Several more charcoals of both Eduardo and his mother lay on the floor, each weighted down by shells and stones. A wrapped package leaned awkwardly against the wall. It was the first time she had seen Michelette at St. Jude's since the fateful night.

Several other students, all former classmates of Eduardo's, swayed with the music. One busily hung a pair of primitive masks on a column. Both had been carved from coconut shells and painted in primary colors. The lower face's bright red mouth grimaced in agony, and its yellow eyeballs, outlined in black, squinted with pain. The upper mask, painted black with facial features outlined in white, exuded happiness. The other students arranged flowers and other greenery and set them on tables.

Someone had placed a table in the center of the shelter. On the makeshift palm frond tablecloth lay a machete, a fishing hand line, a pile of charcoal, and two dolls representing a mother nursing a baby. Hand-fashioned from sugarcane leaves and mango seeds, the dolls, painted with brilliant reds, yellows, blues, and glossy black and white, represented the beauty and glory of life.

On another column hung a painting, amateurish in technique yet unmistakable in meaning. On a blue background, it depicted, in white with black hair-thin strokes, the Virgin Mary standing in prayer side-by-side with the brightly hued red and yellow image of the Maitresse Erzulie, the Vodoun goddess of love.

Pearl, entranced with the aboriginal charm of the painting, heard Sister Joan's rapid shuffle come up behind her. She turned as the nun, in her normal, shrew-type pace, bustled past her balancing, busboy style, a large tray of cookies.

"Beautiful, isn't it?" she asked in her rapid-fire manner while setting the tray on the table and snapping up two cookies. "Natti's having a heyday in the kitchen." Her hands and arms were a study of perpetual motion. "She has three or four dozen more coming out. Says she will be cooking all night."

"Yes, it is beautiful. Strange. When I first came to Haiti, I was turned off by this type of art. Even somewhat scared, particularly of the imagery."

Two of the students helped themselves to cookies. Michelette, oblivious to everyone, continued taping up her charcoals.

"Me, too." Sister Joan said, picking up another baked delight. "I thought that most of the stuff was downright ugly." She bit the cookie in half, chewed rapidly, and swallowed. "I thought I was looking at something directly from the bowels of the devil himself."

Pearl recalled a similar reaction. "Me, too." She succumbed to the tantalizing stack of fattening treats. "Maybe we're just conditioned."

"I don't think so." She put the remaining piece in her mouth and brushed her hands together.

"What, then?" Pearl asked. "This puts their idol on the same level as the Virgin."

"As *our* idol, the Virgin, you mean." Sister Joan picked up another cookie.

Her comment stunned Pearl.

"Shocked?"

"I think so."

"Anyone spiritual worships idols. We just don't realize it. Even an idea that has been concretized is an idol. To me, there is only one God. However, there are as many interpretations of the spirit of God, or, as some say, messengers of God, or angels, or, as Haitians say, Loas, as there are people or groups, and I believe that whatever path a person takes to find their place in the God's universe, go for it." She waved her hand as if blessing everything in the Shelter. "For many Haitians, all this stuff works." She picked up another cookie, turned like a whirlwind, and, in her typical fidgety manner, hurried away, calling over her shoulder, "See you later."

Moland drove the pickup through the open gate and backed up to the shelter. He got out, lowered the tailgate, and lifted a covered barrel to the ground. He beckoned to Pearl. As she approached, she spotted the containers of clear liquid neatly packed and braced in the back of the truck. She started counting.

"Thirty-one gallons," Moland said.

"How many people do you expect?"

"Ultimately, several hundred. Bet we run out, but this is all I could beg, borrow, and steal on such short notice." He picked a jug from the truck and poured it in the barrel. "Hope somebody brings some of their own. How about giving me a hand?"

Pearl began pouring. "I believe this is what you would call a blend?"

"As good as any blended Scotch or Canadian whiskey." He went around, opened the passenger side door, and lifted a big cloth sack from the truck. The sack sounded like a clattering of broken shells as he set it beside the barrel. He laid it open and removed a bunch of dippers; two enameled blue and white, three half-gourds with hooks, and one foggy plastic, and hung each from the rim of the barrel. The remainder of the sack was filled with cups or half bowls, all fashioned from any useable natural material including shells and gourds.

As Pearl emptied the last gallon into the barrel, Moland pulled a small ladle from the sack and stirred. He dipped a bit of the blend into a coconut shell mug and offered it to Pearl. "Oh, why not?" She lifted it to her lips, sipped the sweet, homemade rum, and raised her eyebrows. "Not bad."

Moland sipped from the dipper, smacked his lips, stared into space, then nodded approvingly. "Not the best, but it'll do for the masses."

Pearl started to pour the remainder of her coconut cup back into the barrel. She figured the alcohol content rendered any bacteria she might have harmless. But it had been one hell of a week, she rationalized, so she gulped the remainder.

"Way to go, lady! You're getting to understand yourself."

Pearl dropped the cup back into the sack, walked over to the wall where Michelette had hung her charcoal sketches, and studied the drawings in depth. The first, of course, was the largest; Eduardo sitting on a tree branch. The second portrayed his family. His mother stood beside an open fire, making charcoal. On the other side of the fire stood a little boy and a man. The man held several stalks of sugar cane and a machete; the boy a fish. A large pile of charcoal briquettes surrounded the trio.

It quickly became obvious that Michelette had composed a pictorial of Eduardo's short life. One showed him and his mother standing on the shore waving good-bye to his father. In the distance was a bright white light.

Common to each sketch, the pile of briquettes, like Eduardo, grew while his mother's frail body shrank. In the next to last drawing, Michelette depicted Eduardo as her hero, saving her from a monumental tragedy. In the final drawing, three men, faces shown in great detail, wore the body of Baron Samedi, the Vodoun trafficker of souls; in the background, over open fires, three large, steaming kettles.

Michelette taped the last corner of her final sketch. It portrayed Eduardo and his mother ascending into brightness and approaching his father's outstretched hands. No briquettes. At the bottom of the picture, Michelette and her mother waved good-bye.

"These are wonderful." Pearl choked.

Michelette turned and looked at her through dull, bloodshot eyes. Dried tear streams lined her dusty face. Pearl realized that the dress Michelette wore was the same one she had worn that fateful night. "Thank you." She wiped her hands on her dress. "I think I can sleep now."

Pearl opened her arms. Michelette fell into them and wept.

The Pickup at the International Airport in Port-au-Prince

Francois and Georges waited at the doorway leading into the terminal. As friends of several security guards, they had no trouble getting clearance to wait in the secured area. Georges held a yellow sign with large, red script, "Welcome Wayne and Beverly." None had met before.

The American Airlines jet had landed and taxied to its berth. A set of stairs rolled to the door behind the cockpit. As it opened, an onboard stair lowered from the rear of the plane. Momentarily passengers began filing from both openings. After almost half of the passengers disembarked and lined up at baggage claim, Francois saw a man and woman who came down the back stairs look toward them and smile. The two favored each other. The man, carrying a black, stuffed backpack, had a deep tan and sun-bleached hair. The athletic woman, wearing jeans and red western shirt and rolling a green and black paisley suitcase, had her brunette hair cut short and parted in the middle. Her facial features were strikingly familiar—a young Pearl. From the short distance, Francois could see her tired eyes. As the pair approached, Francois extended her hand to the man. "Wayne Johnson?"

"Yes, and this is my sister, Beverly. Thank you for meeting us."

Georges extended his hand to Wayne. "Georges Jean Charles. We've heard a lot about you both."

"Same here," Wayne replied.

"Do you have any more bags?" Georges asked.

"No," Beverly said.

"Good. Let me have your passports and tickets." Georges handed the sign to Francois. "I'll get us through pretty quick. Follow me."

Georges turned, briskly walked up to the customs cage, and waved the passports. The customs agent behind the glass acknowledged and waved him ahead of the long line. Several people backed up. One mumbled something, and the people in the queue murmured. As Georges motioned the trio through, he turned to the line and said to no one in particular, "Sorry. Emergency. Thanks for allowing us to come through. We appreciate your patience." The murmuring stopped.

At the baggage inspection, the customs agent smiled at Georges and Francois and waved them through, promising to stop by the next time he was up St. Marc way. Georges and Francois muscled their way through the crowd of would-be baggage handlers surrounding the terminal exit and led Wayne and Beverly through a chain-link gate to a car. They quickly exited the airport parking lot, negotiated through heavy traffic while dodging many potholes. When the traffic thinned out and the asphalt was reasonably smooth, he handed the passports and some papers to Francois and asked her to explain.

"You have to keep this yellow certificate with your passport all the time, and turn it in when you leave. Also, remember that you need twenty-five U.S. dollars and ten Haitian gourdes departure tax."

"Wayne's been here several times," Beverly said. "We have the dollars, but have to get the Haitian money."

"I thought as much," Francois said. She dug into her purse and handed each a crisp, new ten gourdes note. "That's only about a dollar and a half U.S. Consider it a gift of appreciation for coming. Your mother's been a godsend to the school. A refreshing beacon of light. When do you fly out?"

"Unfortunately, I have to go back on the eleven-thirty flight Tuesday," Beverly said. "By taking the red-eye special, and, luckily, today being a teacher workday, I was able to make the trip taking only two personal days, that is, providing all return connections go smoothly."

"We think your mom's going to be surprised by the party, and I know she'll almost faint when she sees the two of you."

"I hope our stay doesn't put you out," Wayne said.

"Not at all, as long as you don't mind sharing a shower. We've set up cots for you in my studio. I think you'll find them rather comfortable."

"Right now, I'd find a concrete floor comfortable," Beverly said.

"I'm sure you're tired," Francois said. "If you like, you can take a nap when we get to my place. For tomorrow, we thought we'd take you on a little cruise in one of Georges's boats, and maybe get in a little snorkeling. There's a beautiful, shallow reef about fifteen minutes offshore."

"Sounds great to me," Wayne exclaimed. "I've not been in Haitian waters before."

"Sounds fine to me," Beverly replied.

"We had a tragedy of sorts this week," Georges said.

"What do you mean 'of sorts'?"

Francois responded quickly. "It was a tragedy." The two hosts explained the week's happenings, pausing only to answer the visitors' questions about landmarks and structures along the road.

As they pulled up to the gate into Francois's compound, the artist knew that the four were going to get along splendidly. She punched the button on her remote and the gate, ever so slowly, creaked opened.

The Celebration of Life

Pearl had taken the exhausted Michelette to her room. Showing token resistance, the girl stretched out on Pearl's bed. No sooner had she sat in the rocker than the youngster was fast asleep. Pearl, too, nodded off.

Mournful African chants drifting from the Shelter woke her, but Michelette lay sound asleep, not having moved from her original position. Feeling weighted by Michelette's suffering, Pearl lifted herself from the chair, tiptoed to the basin, and quietly freshened up. In her final routine, she checked to see if the scar showed. It did. As she was applying a bit more foundation, she heard it.

Drums. At first a faint beat. Then, with the drums, the wind carried the coarse, primitive sound from horns. The crowd was coming. As Pearl opened the door, the music grew louder. She turned and looked at the Haitian sleeping beauty. Not a stir.

Along with the deep basses and horns, Pearl heard the high pitch of small, hollow drums and the sharp, crisp notes of wood flutes. She gently closed the door and, joined by the sisters on the shell walk, hurried toward the shelter. The music rose, and the women heard the slapping hands and wooden stick accompaniment. The sad, low groan of a saxophone penetrated deep into her soul. As the teachers rounded the corner of the Louvre, the euphony grew to a double fortissimo. Moland, wearing his dress jacket, opened wide the driveway gate. Father Mike appeared on the top step of the breezeway and rocked with the beat.

Colorful and mostly barefooted, a group of ten to fourteen musicians danced in followed by a mesmerized ragtag crowd swaying with the music, many with their hands raised in the air clapping to the beat. Most men carried small liquid containers. Many women, scattered among the crowd, balanced trays of fruits and breads on their head. Several lofty, homemade banners moved with the crowd. In addition to Creole phrases, each banner had one or more small voodoo symbols and imagery. The most common was the symbol of Legba, the voodoo guardian of the crossroads. Legba, according to ancient mythology, opens the gates to the spiritual world. When depicted as a human, Legba is usually a lame old man with a cane or crutch, but one with great physical and mental strength and endurance. Another prominent banner was that of the Virgin Mary alongside the voodoo goddess of love. It was almost identical to the painting hanging in the Shelter.

Pearl and the sisters watched for what seemed like eternity as the procession passed through the gate. When the final stragglers pranced through, Moland motioned for Pearl and the sisters to join the crowd. People of all colors and manners of dress milled in and around the Shelter while the musicians played. And Moland's barrel was very popular.

Everyone danced or shuffled to the band's catchy rhythm. Pearl clapped her hands, tapped her foot, and swung her hips to the beat, as did the three nuns. Suddenly a happy bellow sounded. The crescendo of the music seemed to shake the ground, and the crowd parted, making room for several pairs of dancers, each interpreting the music in their own way. All but one of the men danced without shirt or shoes, most in ragged-edged cutoffs. Their sinewy bodies glistened with perspiration.

The women wore thin, brilliantly hued blouses and faded, billowing skirts tied with brightly colored bandanas. They, too, were barefoot. As they danced, the music and crowd responded to each new movement. The more sensuous the maneuver, the louder the roar of approval.

A new couple jumped in from the fringe. She raised her hands above her head and twirled like an ice skater, sending her full, red and yellow skirt and hip-length jet black hair flying while her partner danced impromptu movements around her, counter to her rotation. Suddenly they stopped and faced each other. He clapped his hands above his head. She twirled. Simultaneously, he stepped forward, grasped her hips, and held her close as she bent forward at the waist, sending her hair flying over her head, forming a curtain over her face and breasts. While gyrating at the connected hips, she slowly raised up while pulling off her blouse. Her parted hair camouflaged what were no doubt well-formed breasts. Then, in slow, sensuous movements, she circled him while he, swaying and turning in the opposite direction, removed his long-sleeved shirt, tied it to his waist, and braided the sleeves. The crowd roared their approval when he allowed the sleeves to phallically flop in front. Sister Marie gasped and put her hand to her mouth, Sister Ester covered her eyes, and Sister Joan giggled, her eyes glued to the shirtsleeves. After several minutes of dramatic, breathtaking dance, the music subsided and the couples slowed. Two pair left the dance floor and plopped down, exhausted, in the nearest clear space.

Sister Marie and Sister Ester walked toward the Nest shaking their heads. Pearl, wanting to look in on Michelette, followed. The girl slept and, unlike the two nuns, Pearl immediately returned to the Shelter.

The moon hovered directly overhead, and the music played on. The barrel, emptied within two hours of the band's appearance, became a musical instrument. Then Pearl noticed that Moland was gradually making his way to a table in front of where Michelette had taped her interpretations. He propped his cane against the wall, moved a chair in place, and used it to ascend the table. Gradually, the raucous crowd subsided. All faces turned toward the old man. The musicians, all but the drums, stopped playing, but kept their seats. The drummers, using cutoff palm brushes, simulated wind rustling through trees.

Moland waved one hand and the lights dimmed and blackened. Shadows with torches surrounded the Shelter. The crowd murmured, and the barely perceptive drum wind increased in tempo. A horn player moaned through a large conch shell. A procession of torchbearers snaked through the crowd and up to Michelette's sketch wall, each taking up a position beside a drawing. The crowd shuddered, then stood motionless and stared at Moland. The instrumentalist groaned.

His eyes on Moland, Father Mike crept up beside Pearl and whispered. "Watch this man work."

Sister Joan joined the two and mumbled. "This will be a marvelous show."

Backlit by the torches, Moland, wearing his jacket with slightly padded shoulders, presented a dramatic image. As the saxophone moaned a low cry, he made a broad, swooping motion with one arm, then his hand shot into mid-air and grasped a writhing snake. The crowd cheered. He held the serpent above his head and waved it back and forth. With everyone's eyes glued to the serpent, Moland, just as dramatically, reached up and grabbed a second. The crowd yelled and jumped up and down, clapping their hands above their heads. He held both thrashing creatures above his head while shouting something in Creole.

Father Mike whispered. "Damballah, the snake god of voodoo tradition, is seldom used, but Moland has perfected its effect and everyone loves it."

Moland pointed a serpent to the first sketch and spoke, holding the snakes in front. The drawing's torch bearing guardian held his flame close; its shadows on the sketches brought goose bumps.

Father Mike said, "Eduardo is a hero. Like Damballah, his spirit is as strong as the python. Even though his body is now gone, his spirit is in the company of God, as are the spirits of his mother and father."

Moland's attention turned to the next sketch, as did its torchbearer and the crowd's attention. The shaman spoke with a deep, penetrating mystical voice.

Father Mike interpreted; "His father, a strong, dedicated man, died trying to find a better life on earth for his family, unlike many men who, for no reason, abandon their families, they will never stop suffering. And the boy's poor mother dedicated her life to the hero, therefore is a hero herself. When her reason to live departed this life, so did her spirit. She will become like Aida-Wedo and be one of Damballah's wives." Moland waved the snakes.

The crowd roared its approval. Several started to dance in place, and the musicians played louder and faster. But Moland's voice still reigned supreme as he used each sketch to paint a wonderful, touching memorial to Eduardo and his mother.

Sister Joan explained. "Damballah is a good, strong Loa, a very influential spirit in this part of Haiti. We have angels in our mythology, they have various Loa, or spirits, because that is something to which they can relate. To be with Damballah is the same as being in heaven with God. To be married to a spirit, or angel, is about as high an honor as a woman can have." She looked at Pearl. "Kind of like being married to the Holy Spirit."

The spirits, and the decibel level of music and shouting, rose as Moland continued to extol the virtues of Eduardo and his mother. Finally, Moland jumped off the table, his limp no longer apparent, hopped and danced to the corner of the Shelter, knelt and released the serpents, then rose and, clapping his hands above his head, motioned for several to join him. They created a line that, as the band played, weaved its way around the Shelter. The line grew, including many of the perimeter torchbearers, and gradually made its way by Pearl. The bearers beside Michelette's sketches stood in place. When it came time to join in, Father Mike grasped the hips of the woman at the end. A Haitian woman grasped him, then Sister Joan joined. Two more Haitians quickly attached themselves.

"What the hell," Pearl thought. She grabbed the hips of a masculine Haitian and joined the swaying, snaking procession as it slithered to nowhere in particular.

Only when Moland turned and led the animated, chanting line back along side her and winked did she realize that he was in total control; every move was calculated. The cagey old man led the line such that all got a close look at Michelette's interpretation of Eduardo's life. One woman screamed and fainted. A man fell to the ground and writhed like a fishing worm. Several others broke out and danced.

Pearl, in a sudden epiphany, realized that all explanations of things unknown are based upon the limited understanding of those to whom the explanations are made, and that to try to have an explanation of God is to put a limit on that which is limitless.

Moland led the procession from the Shelter, and, as if he had planned it, a sudden rain shower drenched the people but not their spirit. Both Pearl and Sister Joan stepped out of line and, faces raised to the sky, enjoyed the heavy, warm downpour. As suddenly as it appeared, it stopped, and the cloud moved off. Again, the stars twinkled and the moon glowed.

As she stood looking up, soaked to the skin, she understood what her own daughter had been trying to tell her, that all rules of personal conduct are made by people, or groups of people, not God.

She made her decision.

How the drummers could keep playing, Pearl didn't know. The crowd gradually thinned. Most wandered, solo or in pairs, through the driveway gate. Several, hand in hand, strolled up the path toward the back gate. As she watched a couple faded into the shadows, Moland sidled up beside her. "Better stay on the paths tonight."

"I think you're right. That was a wonderful service, Moland. Where did you get the snakes?"

"Did you understand what was going on?"

"Father Mike and Sister Joan explained as you spoke. You had the crowd mesmerized."

Moland grinned. "There's a little magician in all of us."

"More in some than others, I would say. What about the snakes?"

"Sorry. Trade secret." His eyes glistened as a broad smile creased his dark face.

"And the limp?"

He shrugged his shoulders. "It comes and goes." He walked to the wall, retrieved his cane, and limped back.

"You're a sly one."

"Yes, I am." His eyes narrowed. "But I think you have something to say."

"I've made a decision."

Moland nodded. "Are you going to join the living?"

"I hope so."

"So do I, Pearl. So do I." Cane in hand, he hobbled off and disappeared around the corner where he had released the snakes.

Suddenly, even though fifty or so people still moved to the music, she felt alone. Sister Joan and Father Mike sat on a bench talking.

But she was really lonely. Not for her kids, not for anyone at the school, not for anyone in particular. Just lonely. If being alive meant feeling so isolated, perhaps her decision wasn't so good. Maybe she *was* committing a mortal sin.

As the eastern sky began to brighten, the last drumbeat sounded, and Moland, as only he could, conjured up an earthen jug of clarin. The band passed it around until it was empty, then gathered their instruments and straggled off. The Vodoun priest was the last to leave. When he got to the gate, he turned, waved, then shuffled into the foliage.

It had been a wonderful celebration of life, and, for the Haitians, a joyful respite from the daily chore of living.

The End of the Beginning

The Fateful Saturday

When Pearl lay down at dawn, she had immediately fallen asleep. In the throws of waking up, she turned and buried her face in the pillow. She sniffed. She opened her eyes and sniffed again. She raised her head, looked at the pillow, lowered her nose to the pillow's surface, and took a big whiff. Unmistakably a man's aroma.

A male's smell? Oh, yes. She easily recalled the odors of the only man with whom she had shared a bed. The body odors. The farts. The bad breath. And other women's perfumes.

But this was a tantalizing, musky fragrance. She laughed. Then it dawned on her. She felt good, but more important, she felt alive. She was really happy and had no guilt feelings whatsoever. Burying her face in the pillow and wrapping it around her head, she giggled like a little girl who had just gotten away with some mischievous prank. Suddenly she stopped laughing and, with one eye, peeked from the pillow and scanned the unfamiliar room. Where was she? Then she remembered! Primal Hall's guest room. Her eyes darted to the window. It was bright outside. She wondered what time it was.

Sitting up, she looked around, then realized that she was naked. For no reason, she pulled the bed sheet up to her neck. Good thing she didn't get up in a daze and wander to where the bathroom should have been. She would have wound up in the living room. Her clothes hung over the one chair and the foot of the bed. The room had no clock. She wrapped the sheet around herself as she stood and clumsily stretched while walking to the window. A glance skyward confirmed her assumption that it was, indeed, late morning. Oh, well. It had been a long, fun night. *These Haitians sure know how to have a good time.* She checked her clothes. They were not quite dry but would have to do.

Pearl dressed, shivering as the damp clothing touched her skin, then spread the bed and made a final self-check in the mirror above the chest of drawers. She looked awful. She ran fingers through her hair to give the stringy, mussed stuff a degree of order and hoped most of the staff wouldn't see her. But she knew Natti would have coffee ready, and probably something else, so she stopped by the kitchen, fetched a cup of brew, and went to check on Michelette and take a bath. Stepping onto the shell walk, she glanced at the empty Shelter, then headed toward the Nest. The rain shower had washed everything clean. The flowers sparkled as water dripped from their petals. Two butterflies circled in their mating ritual. It was indeed a beautiful day.

Sister Joan, tending the hybrid daffodils, looked up as Pearl approached. "Wonderful party, wasn't it?" A cup of coffee and a plate of cookies lay nearby.

"Yes, it was. You look refreshed. I believe you were still up when I went to bed."

"Father Mike and I talked a lot last night." She reached for the plate and extended it to Pearl. "Have one?"

"Thank you. Is Michelette still asleep?"

"I've been up for a couple of hours and haven't seen or heard a thing."

Pearl quietly opened the door and peeked in. Michelette looked as if she had not moved. She quietly closed the door. "She's still asleep."

"Is she sick?" Sister Joan asked.

"No. I bet this is the first time she's slept since Eduardo died."

"What?"

"If I know her, she probably didn't eat much either. Well, I have to slip in and get some dry clothes. May I use your shower?"

"Go light on the water," Joan said, finishing the last cookie. "In spite of the rain, we're still low. Moland took some to several families yesterday."

Pearl tiptoed barefoot into her room, garnered from the wardrobe her sky-blue sun dress with large white flowers, fresh underwear, a towel, washcloth, and soap then glided to the door. Michelette stirred and rolled over. The girl would soon wake up and be hungry.

In Sister Joan's shower, Pearl turned the faucet, soaked her thinning washcloth while letting the cool water dampen her body, then turned the water off. She soaped up and scrubbed, turned the water back on, quickly rinsed, then off. Total time in the shower was no longer than three minutes. She felt refreshed. As she dried off and put on her clothes, she heard voices from outside. Combing her hair, she opened the door and saw Sister Joan talking with Michelette's mother. Both women looked at Pearl.

"Good morning," Pearl said.

Michelette's mother smiled and returned the greeting.

"She became concerned when Michelette didn't come home last night and came looking for her," Sister Joan explained. "She thought she might be here. She brought a dress for her to change." The nun held out a rolled-up dress. "You were right. Since Eduardo's death, all she did was work on the drawings."

"I assume you told her that Michelette was in my room?"

Sister Joan nodded. "She's relieved and wants to let her sleep. We were discussing Michelette's work when you came out."

"I don't think she was at the memorial, was she?"

Sister Joan turned and, in Creole, asked the question.

Michelette's mom shook her head and spoke fast and rather lengthily.

Sister Joan paused before interpreting. "She had to work last night or would have lost her best-paying job."

"I'll take her to the Shelter."

The Computers

Bob, driving Franck's sport utility, drove to Ben Alce's place in an industrial park near the old military airport and found the front security gate locked. He checked his watch. Eleven o'clock, the designated time. Where was Ben? All Bob could do was wait. He hoped there had not been a glitch.

At eleven forty-five, Ben drove up, and jumped out of his car. "I'm sorry, Bob," he said, unlocking the gate. "I made the mistake of coming through town because it is usually the quickest way, but I got caught in a major demonstration and couldn't get through."

"Good thing I came over and down Route Del Mas then. What was it about this time?"

"The teachers, nurses, and doctors who work for the government. Some told me they hadn't been paid in over three months."

Bob was well aware of the conditions and knew that demonstrations, particularly by government workers, were one of Haiti's national pastimes. And usually for good reason.

"I put my car in neutral and was pushed along by the crowd until I found an opening." Ben held the gate open. "Can you pull around back?"

Bob drove around the building, backed to the loading platform, got out, and waited.

Ben opened the back door. "We have it all set aside in here," he said, propping the door open. "I haven't checked it yet."

They checked off the equipment as each box was loaded. Four monitors, five five-hundred megahertz

computers, each with a CD-ROM drive, super 3 ½"
drive, and 54.4 baud modem, one external zip drive,
one external read/write CD-ROM, and four ink-jet
printers.

"They can use the existing computer to store files.
We threw in a twelve-station network hub and installed
network cards in each computer," Ben said. He handed
Bob a large roll of wire and a package. "Here's the
network cable. Connections are in the bag, along with
a connection tool, compliments of the Rotary Club of
Port-au-Prince. Does the school have high speed
Internet access?"

"Don't know. Only over the phone lines, I
suspect."

"We'll have to work with them on that," Ben said.
"Could take awhile way out there."

"It would be nice. How about cellular?"

"Very expensive here in Haiti, but I'll work out
something."

Bob signed the bill and got in the Ford. "Meet you
around front."

He left the compound, turned onto Dessalines
Boulevard, and drove toward destiny.

Francois's La Petite

"What a beautiful place to live!" Beverly
exclaimed as she and Francois stood neck deep in the
water just off the beach. The cloudless sky, mountains
in the background, palm trees, and crystal-clear water
presented an idyllic setting.

"The place was abandoned when I came across it,"
Francois said. "Even Georges thought I was crazy to
buy it. No available drinking water. Ground wouldn't
grow much because of all the dumped waste products
over the years. Some people even said it was haunted."

"I sense an interesting story behind that."

"Somewhat. Kinda like a microcosm of Haiti itself,
I guess. Anyway it's lucky for me. The people that are
hung up on such things won't come near La Petite. But
the best I can understand, the house is over four
hundred years old. I found some dated Spanish and
French coins in the bottom of the pit."

"Wow!"

"In the seventeen hundreds, it became an aloe
plantation. You know, where they cultivated aloe
plants and processed them for oil. That's the fire pit
between the house and studio, which used to be the
barn and processing factory."

"So what's this haunted business?"

"There were several slave uprisings before Haiti
became independent in the early eighteen hundreds. It
seems that the commandeur, or overseer, fathered by
the French owner on one of his visits from Paris, was
rather ruthless. He, like everyone else, controlled by
fear. More than one slave was dipped in boiling aloe

oil, and, if a slave woman refused his advances, she would be strung up and skinned alive."

"Yuck! That's awful."

"According to history, that kind of treatment was common. It's estimated that at one time that there were about one hundred fifty thousand Blancs and Mulattos—that's whites and those of mixed blood—and over a million slaves here in Haiti. Practicality dictated ruling by power, force, and fear. In the seventeen hundreds, it took over twenty thousand slaves a year just to replace those lost to death and desertion."

Beverly whistled.

"Anyway, during the war for independence, apparently Toussaint Louverture's forces—kinda Haiti's George Washington—came through here on their way to Port-au-Prince and freed the slaves. When the troops left, the slaves decided to take their revenge instead of giving the overseer and his family safe haven to Cap Haitian as ordered. The three children were lucky. They were simultaneously decapitated while their parents watched. Then, according to oral tradition, the slaves hit the rum and things got really nasty. The overseer was strung between two poles, disrobed, and had a long, sharpened stick shoved in his rectum and hammered until it finally came out his throat. They say he was still breathing when the stick was pulled back in and rerouted through his mouth. Then they put him over an open pit and roasted him. But the worst came to his wife, a former slave, who was almost as cruel as he. She, well along with child, was strapped to a cross, eyelids stitched open, hoisted

231

in the air, and forced to watch her husband being impaled. When he was put over the fire, they cut off his penis and stuffed it in her mouth, then split her birth canal open with a machete. The fetus dropped and hung loose while she slowly bled to death."

"Oh, my God!"

"According to the legend, Toussaint's officers heard her wail on the wind. The troop returned and slaughtered all the slaves because they had disobeyed his orders to give the family safe haven."

"And?"

"And today, some natives say that when the moon and wind are just right, they can still hear the wails of the dying woman and slaves."

"And the haunt?"

"So the story goes, they dropped the slaves' bodies into the well. That's why, I'm told, that the water is no good."

"Do you believe that?"

"The history and the bloodshed, yes. That was very common in Haiti during those times. That's why historians say that Haiti's history is written in blood. About the water, no. It's just heavily polluted surface water, but if the legend keeps out the thieves and intruders, who am I to dispute it?" She dipped beneath the surface and came up face first.

"I can't imagine that people still believe the haunted story and the legend of the bad water," Beverly said. "Not in the twentieth century."

"Between 70 and 80 percent of the adult Haitian population is illiterate." She lay back and floated on the surface. "But that's slowly changing, thanks to people like your mother. I've seen a difference just in the last ten years. Haiti, in its own way and time, will get there."

A chugging engine turned their heads seaward. Georges's boat rounded the point. Wayne waved from the bow, and the women returned the gesture. Georges slowed the engine and brought the vessel close, Wayne secured a ladder to the side. Francois followed Beverly aboard. As Francois's feet hit the deck, Georges pushed the throttle and headed seaward.

"We'll be at the reef in a few minutes," he called. Then he saw something on the horizon, shaded his eyes from the glare, and peered into the distance. "Look there. A whale!"

All looked, and sure enough, a whale played on the surface. "Let's go take a look."

Wayne leaped beside Georges. "Are they common?"

"Let's say they're uncommon this time of year. They're making a comeback so we're not getting too close."

The two couples enjoyed watching the whale breach and loll on the surface. In spite of all three pleading for a closer look, Georges dropped anchor just off the reef, well away from the large mammal. While Georges stayed aboard, the trio enjoyed the beauty of a Caribbean coral reef.

She Finally Wakes Up

Michelette sat up and stretched. Her back ached. The sun indicated that it was well past noon. She started to spread the bed and noticed her rolled-up dress lying across the foot. Her mother, her wonderful, patient, understanding mother, had come looking for her with a clean dress. How could she ever be in conflict with such love? She felt a pang of guilt because of the testing confrontation.

But the party! And what happened to the sculpture she had brought with her? She hurriedly enjoyed the luxury of a brief shower in Mrs. Johnson's bathroom, dressed, and stepped outside. Mrs. Johnson and Sister Joan, beside the Louvre, were picking up small bits of trash.

Mrs. Johnson looked up. "Well, look who has joined the land of the living."

"Good afternoon," Sister Joan said. "We were just talking about whether or not we should wake you."

Michelette walked to them feeling refreshed. "Is Mama still here?"

"She's taking a nap in my room," Sister Joan said. "Came here about midday. She was worried."

"I know," Michelette looked at the ground and kicked a rock. "I'm afraid I've been hard to live with."

"That's what she said," Sister Joan replied.

234

"I'll have to make it up to her somehow. I was really mean to her. And everybody, I suppose."

"Let's just say you weren't your normal self," Mrs. Johnson said. "But, after what you've been through, few could blame you."

"That's not an excuse. I'm still the one responsible for how I act. Sorry I missed the celebration. How was it?"

"Wonderful," the teachers said in unison.

"And Moland built his words around your drawings."

"I didn't mean for him to do that. They were just my way of dealing with everything. Where are they?"

"Oh," Mrs. Johnson said, "they're still taped to the wall. No one dared touch them."

"I'll go take them down now, and I have to find something." She was really worried about the package she had brought. It was the special sculpture for Mrs. Johnson. She wouldn't normally have scaled Francois's wall, but she had not been thinking straight. Anyway, now she had to find it. And she also had to get word to Francois that she had it. She had really created a messy situation.

"If it's the package of school work you brought," Sister Joan said, winking at Michelette, "Father Mike has it. He saw you lay it at the base of the wall and, knowing that you were preoccupied, took it into Primal Hall."

Michelette got the message. Now she had to turn her attention to getting word to Francois, otherwise the artist would be turning her studio upside down, and would be furious when she found out what happened.

Michelette had seen Francois lose her cool. It wasn't a pretty sight.

"Well, I think I'll take the sketches down and go over to Francois's and burn them."

"What?" Mrs. Johnson exclaimed. "Why burn them? They're wonderful."

"But they are also private, and mine. No. The only way is to burn them." Michelette walked toward the shelter.

"What about your mother?" Mrs. Johnson asked. "If I recall, she doesn't approve of you being at Francois's."

Michelette had forgotten about that. "Just tell her that I'll be back in about an hour, and to wait for me. We'll go home together."

Michelette went to the Shelter and began to take down the first drawing when Jean Claude and Girard, two of her classmates, walked up. Their pockets bulged, and Michelette saw the end of a wrapped package sticking from Girard's pocket. A present for Mrs. Johnson.

"Wait a minute," Jean Claude said.

"Can't we see them?" Girard asked. That was the very first time that quiet, troubled Girard Louis had expressed any interest in anything but guns, knives, and computers. Michelette looked at the two of them, said yes, and backed away. As they were looking at the third sketch, two more classmates wandered through the gate and over to the Shelter wall.

"Everybody in St. Marc is talking about these and the party last night," one said.

"Weren't you here?" Jean Claude asked.

"We were," Girard said proudly. "You should have seen Moland pull those snakes out of the air. That was wild!"

Three more students, each carrying a package, wandered in, and looked at the drawings while listening to the two boys describe in detail the party. Michelette decided to leave the drawings on the wall and head over to Francois's just as Moland limped up, accompanied by Father Mike.

"I believe I have something of yours," the priest said.

Michelette looked to make sure Mrs. Johnson wasn't nearby. "I climbed the wall at Francois's and got it. I've got to go tell her."

"Not to worry," Father Mike said. "I told her I had it. She was a little surprised, but I think she understood, as we all do. How are you?"

For the first time since the incident, she felt totally relieved. She had mourned through the sketches, then felt apprehensive because of going by Francois's and getting the gift for Mrs. Johnson. Finally that little escapade was resolved. The past couple of days had been a bad dream. Then she remembered the concluding lines of her poem. "I'm fine, Father. Just fine."

She turned and joined her classmates.

It All Comes Together

It was an hour before the time of the party, and Moland had volunteered to get Pearl off the grounds for a little bit. After all, it was supposed to be a surprise. Still wearing his only dress jacket, he limped over to Pearl and pulled her aside. The knowing Sister Joan, obvious to Moland but not Pearl, stepped back so as not to hear. "You asked about the snakes. Want to know more?"

"Are you up to one of your jokes?"

"No, ma'am. Not this time. It's just that you expressed an interest, so I thought I'd show you. Besides, I have to get some water to a family who has a child down with something and I would like some company."

"That's more like it. Snakes, indeed."

Moland and Pearl gathered four plastic gallon jugs from the kitchen, went to the main cistern and filled them, put them in the pickup, and drove out of the compound toward Michelette's path. He was going the long way because he didn't want to pass by Bob Turner, who should be bringing the computers in about now.

"That was some show you put on last night," Pearl said. "How and when did you orchestrate the lights going out, the torches, and the music? It came off rather professionally."

Moland snuffed, pretending that he'd been insulted. "Well, I never."

"Oh, give me a break," Pearl said, gently slapping the old man on the shoulder. "You know what I mean."

"I just read the crowd, talked with a few people, and let it flow. I didn't orchestrate anything. All I did was figure out what was going on and bend and mold my message to fit. I had no idea what I was going to say until I saw the girl's drawings, then it all came together. And if you recall, the generator went off at its normal time. I just watched the clock and prepared the torchbearers. Naturally, I asked the ones ahead of time to stand by the sketches." The truck hit a bump and both left their seats. "Oh, didn't see that one." He slowed the vehicle. "Are you okay?"

"Yes. Now what about the snakes?"

Moland shot his arm out toward her and a snake jumped from his sleeve. Pearl fell against the door and screamed. Then Moland held it still. It was a toy.

"You son of a gun! You scared me half to death."

"Realistic, isn't it? Now put this together with the dim flickering torches, the bootleg rum, the music, the mood, and me waving my arms. It works beautifully." They turned off the main road onto not much more than a path, and slowly bumped along.

"But they're fake."

"Aren't all religious symbols fake? It's the meaning behind the symbol and the emotions invoked that is important, not the symbol itself. I have yet to see a crucifix that was real, and I don't want to, just like I would prefer not to see a real snake."

"Does anyone else know about these toys?"

"Of course. Most worshipers know the snakes are not real, and Father Mike and Sister Joan have known for a long time. The other two sisters, I think, prefer not to know, which is too bad. Now, I believe you said you had made a decision. Want to tell me about it?"

Before Pearl could gather her thoughts, Moland turned into the sand yard of a small but clean stone house painted bright blue. It had an open door and two small, screenless windows on the front. Four children played in the yard. The littlest, probably no more than two, was naked. The biggest, who was maybe six or seven, wore a very old pair of short pants. The others wore not much more than loincloths, and all were barefooted.

Moland opened the map compartment and took out some dried fruit soaked in cane syrup. "How about giving this to the kids while I take the water inside and say a few words to the woman. The oldest child is apparently very sick."

The children were clean, but the little one, a girl, had a bulging stomach, thin legs, and a bright smile. The others stared curiously as Pearl got out of the truck. She switched to her passable Creole. "How are you?"

"Okay," the little girl said. The others just looked.

"Would you like some of this?" Pearl said, sticking her hand into the bag and pulling out a handful of the fruit and offering it in an open palm. The little girl looked at the food, picked out a piece of pineapple, stuck it in her mouth, chewed, swallowed, put her finger to her mouth, and smiled. Pearl's heart melted.

She made an offering to the others, and each cautiously took a piece. Then she started over. This time, they weren't so bashful. They lightened up and began chattering like the kids they were. Their daddy, according to the older one, who turned out to be nine, was working in Port-au-Prince and came home only on the weekends, and then only when he could catch a ride. Their mother made charcoal to sell, and their older brothers worked in the cane fields and fished along the coast. Pearl was shocked to hear that a man, his wife, and eight children lived in this little place.

Moland came from the house, followed by a woman who looked barely strong enough to carry her own weight, much less the baby in her arms. He pulled a bag from behind the seat of the truck, gave it to the frail woman, and said something to her so fast Pearl did not understand. Then he turned to her. "Give them the whole bag, then let's go home."

Pearl handed the bag to the oldest child, who followed his mother into the little house as Pearl and Moland got in, backed out of the yard, and jostled back to the main road.

"That was sad," Pearl said.

"Typical in the country, but they're better off here than in Port-au-Prince. The sick one will die pretty soon."

"What about the others?"

"If all goes as usual, one of the two small ones will die before they're five. Normally, if they survive past that, they will be in it for the long haul."

"What about the one that's sick?"

"Oldest child. A girl, maybe nineteen. Went to Port-au-Prince. Has an advanced case of AIDS."

"How devastating that must be to the mother."

"That's only half of it. The girl, probably a prostitute, was always bringing and sending money

241

home. Now that source has been cut out. They didn't have much in the house to eat. The two oldest boys were expected to bring some food back today." He paused. "And they are one of the better off families in this area."

Pearl and Moland rode awhile in silence.

"There must be more we can do."

"You're helping the best way possible."

"How's that? I feel so inadequate."

"Teaching. Only through literacy can we cure Haiti's problems. The main issue is that many Haitians don't understand the concept of planning for tomorrow. Today is it." He paused. "That's wonderful for peace of mind, but these days it's terrible for society as a whole." As St. Jude's came into view, he closed. "One day, through education, the majority of the Haitians will decide collectively that they must work together to improve their situation. Until that time, political instability will rule." He looked at Pearl. "You're helping much more than you'll ever know, and it really is appreciated."

The remark tore at Pearl's heart. She almost broke into tears as they drove through the gate at St. Jude's. She composed herself when she saw the crowd at the Shelter. "What's the occasion?"

"I don't know," Moland said. "Let's go see."

As they got out of the truck, Pearl saw the sign.

Happy Third Anniversary, Mrs. Johnson

Stunned, Pearl braced herself against the truck with one hand and covered her mouth with the other. She felt tears swelling. She composed herself and looked at Moland. "You sneaky old man."

"Just doing what comes natural." He smiled. "Happy anniversary. We're glad to have you in Haiti." And, for the first time since she had been there, he hugged her. Then he tugged her arm. "Come on, we have a few more surprises."

Everyone began clapping as Moland escorted her to the Shelter. It was all she could do to keep from breaking out in joyful tears. Almost there, the crowd parted, and she saw them. Beverly and Wayne! Pearl lost what little control she had, clasped her hands over her mouth and nose, and just stood looking at them, tears streaming from her eyes. Beverly, eyes turning redder by the second, rushed to and embraced her mother, and Wayne put his arms around both.

Through blurry eyes, Pearl brushed tears from her cheeks as she scanned the crowd, her children's arms still on her shoulders. Best she could tell, most of her students over the past three years were there, along with many parents, and, of course, the staff as well as Francois and Georges. Even obstinate Girard was there, smiling along with the rest. Then she stared at Wayne. "I ought to shoot you for not letting on last week." She grasped his hand and squeezed it. Then she looked at her daughter. "Bev, I . . ."

Michelette stepped forward and took Pearl's hand. "Come on, we have some presents for you."

Jim Henry

As she passed the staff, Pearl asked no one
specifically, "Okay, whose bright idea was this?"

They all chuckled and, in their own version of a
comedy routine, pointed back and forth at each other.
Finally, Sister Marie spoke up. "I guess you have to
blame us all, including the students."

Michelette, joined by several classmates, dragged
Pearl to a table where all the computers, plus some
presents from students, were stacked. She glanced
around and there stood Bob Turner, watching from the
edge of the crowd. He smiled and nodded. Her heart
skipped. Was she going to have to make another
decision?

Someone turned on the boom box and the theme
from *The Sound of Music* filled the air. Recalling the
evening before, she almost laughed at the switch in
tempo. As she opened the presents, the staff, along
with Wayne and Beverly, explained, with help from all
within ear shot, the logistics of the appreciation party
coming together.

Almost all the presents were made by the students
themselves: a little flute carved from a small hollow
piece of wood, a shell necklace made with fishing line,
a stone letter opener, a sunset painted on a large
clamshell, a pencil holder created from the shell of a
coconut, and many other similar gifts that only a
teacher or mother could treasure. The CD in the boom
box changed to *West Side Story*, and Pearl continued to
open presents. A handful of students helped the staff
bring out some food and punch. Just as "Tonight,
Tonight" ended, Father Mike turned off the music,
stood on a chair, and spread his arms, silencing the

crowd. He asked all to stand and bow their head for a word of prayer, concluding with, "And Lord, we especially thank you for sending to us a truly dedicated person, Pearl Johnson."

Pangs of guilt ravaged her body. Only she knew that, if she stuck with her decision, she might not be here much longer. Now they had to go and honor her. How could she possibly desert the school now, particularly for her own selfishness? She put her elbows on the table, covered her face, and hid the tears.

"Now," Father Mike said in the resounding voice of a preacher, "let the guest of honor and her family be first in the food line."

Beverly put her arms around her mother. "Come on, Mom. Everyone understands."

Pearl rose, knowing that no one understood. But, as she should, she let them think she was crying from happiness. That was no doubt part of it. But inside she was miserable. Here she was, ready to sign the divorce papers that had been sitting for more than two years in the bottom of her dresser drawer, at last freeing herself, then Father Mike insinuated that the Church might no longer sanction her being on the staff at St. Jude's, and now this party in her honor. What an emotional roller coaster.

She didn't feel much like eating but took some of the food anyway. When she sat down, Natti brought her a full plate of fried bananas. "Now don't you eat too many."

Pearl almost lost her composure again, but Moland placed a glass of fruit juice in front of her. "This will cheer you up."

She looked at the kind old man. "I'll just bet it will." He grinned, glanced at Bob Turner, and walked off.

"Surprised you, didn't they?" Beverly asked between more well wishers.

"Boy, I'll say. But . . ." Several more students came by and thanked her before she could finish any sentence. "But I guess what I have to say will have to wait."

After everyone had thanked her for being there, she finally turned to her daughter.

This was something she had to do, regardless of the consequences. For the moment, it was only Pearl and her children. This was the time. "Beverly. Wayne." She clasped a hand of each. "I have a confession to make. I've made a decision. An important one." She hesitated, then sighed. This was hard. She looked first at Wayne, then Beverly. "I finally understand what you have been telling me all these years." She paused, choking back a good cry. "It took coming to Haiti and being among these people to teach me what my own daughter has been trying to show me. Anyway, I have been wrong, and I wanted you to know."

Beverly and Wayne looked at each other. Finally, Wayne spoke. "Is that what you have to say?"

"No. This is not easy for me, so please be patient. I have always loved both of you."

"We know that, Mom," Beverly said. "We've always loved you, too."

"Well." She paused. This was it. She had to do it. She had to take another step down her own path. She took a deep breath. "I've decided to give your father his divorce."

She looked at her children. Both appeared to be in shock. Then she went on to explain in simple terms what had led to the decision and the turmoil inside her because she might not be allowed to teach at St. Jude's any longer.

"Well," Beverly finally said, "I think it's about time, and if they decide not to let you come back here and teach because of that, it wasn't meant to be, so let it go. Your being here has served its purpose."

"I agree with Bev, Mom. I know it's hard, but the right thing often is."

The boom box struck up a set of songs from the fifties and sixties. Pearl felt a tap on her shoulder. She turned and looked into Bob's eyes. "I believe that's a tune we danced to just last week. Care to give it another try?"

Pearl, the weight of the decision off her shoulders, almost leaped from her chair. "Why, I'd love to." She took Bob's hand and followed him to the center of the Shelter, oblivious that no one else was dancing. She followed his gentle leads and her natural feelings, missing very few steps. Out of the corner of her eye, she noticed that Georges and Francois, and Beverly and Wayne had joined them on the floor, as well as some parents.

"Almost like you've been taking lessons," Bob said. "You dance beautifully."

"Thank you." She felt her whole body smile. The freedom of her decision was making its effect known.

"The computers paled in comparison to the honors your students have given you."

"Not really," she said as that particular tune concluded. "You don't know how much those computers are going to mean to this school. When the word gets out, we'll be bursting at the seams with students. Some parents will probably come. Would you like to join us at our table?"

"Yes, thank you. Care for some more punch?"

"I think so. But do you know what's in it?" Still clasping a hand, she led him back to the table and picked up her cup.

"I can guess. I saw that older man over there, the one who invited me back this weekend, pouring a bottle into it."

They each took a cup of the happy juice, and as they strolled back to the table, between comments of appreciation to Pearl by others, Bob explained about the computers.

The glow inside her wasn't from the liquid spirits.

* * *

Bev and Wayne were talking to a group that included Francois and Georges. Beverly leaned over and, where only Wayne and Francois could hear, asked, "Hey, bro, who's the man with Mom?"

"Name's Bob Turner. We met him last weekend in the hotel at Port-au-Prince."

"Well, looks to me like she's floating on that cloud nine she used to tell us about."

Wayne studied the pair. "Give me a break. They're just talking."

"He may be talking," Francois said, "but she's doing more than just listening. I think she's reeling him in."

"So do I," Beverly said.

"Ah, come on, Bev. That's Mom."

"You're right, but that's also a woman." She paused. "A free one, at that."

"Not yet," Wayne declared.

"In her heart, she is," Beverly said, "and that's where it counts. We have to get out of the way. As long as we stick around, she'll feel obligated to be with us." Beverly turned to Francois. "Do you have any ideas?"

"Give Georges and me a couple of minutes. We'll come up with something."

* * *

The CD stopped, and, before it could be changed, Father Mike stood on his chair again. "Listen up, everyone. We all know why we're here. We have something special to present to Mrs. Johnson, and we want to give it to her before it gets too late. Francois. Michelette. You're on."

The artist and her protégé came forward and presented to Pearl the package she had seen leaning against the wall.

"Mrs. Johnson," Michelette began. "All of us wanted to give you something special, but didn't know what to do, so everybody said for Francois and me to come up with a piece of art that you could hang in that empty place on the wall in your room and, if you ever leave, which not one of us wants, you can take it with you."

The words cut Pearl to the core, given the decision she had already made. If she had not been sitting down, she would have collapsed. As it was, she leaned against Bob.

Bob steadied her. "Are you okay?"

Biting her bottom lip, she nodded and gripped his hand. She trembled.

"Anyway, we hope you like it." The girl placed the heavy present on the table.

Pearl unwrapped the piece of art, studied it, read the inscription, grabbed Bob's hand, and started crying. He pulled a handkerchief and handed it to her.

* * *

The school's Catholic staff stood on the edge of the crowd. "I can't imagine her liking that awful thing," Sister Marie said. "I don't think I'll even be comfortable with it hanging in the same building."

"I think it's both beautiful and spiritual," said Sister Joan.

"It's ugly," chimed in Sister Ester, shaking her shoulders. "Gives me the willies."

"It is an expression with great meaning," commented Father Mike. "I like it."

* * *

Finally composing herself, Pearl said, "Thanks to both of you. Thanks so much." She recalled all this week's emotional ups and downs. "You have no idea what it means to me, particularly at this time. I will always treasure it." Pearl turned to the crowd. "And thank all of you for trusting in these two. They came up with the right thing at the right time." Pearl pecked both on the cheek. "And, while I have the floor, I want to express my appreciation to all of you for the honor of this gathering, the presents, and especially for bringing to me on this special occasion my two children, Wayne and Beverly. She motioned to them, and glanced at Moland, who lifted his cup in salute. "Now, everyone, thank you for such a wonderful party. Eat, drink, dance, and have a good time." She stopped. "But," she yelled, "get all the kids here on time Monday. Thanks to Mr. Bob Turner," she motioned toward him, "we now have computers!"

An instantaneous applause exploded from the audience, and the music again picked up tempo. Bob held out his hand. "Shall we?"

"Before you two hit the dance floor," Francois said, "I have a suggestion. Pearl, we know that you want to be with Beverly and Wayne, but Club Med has a good disco group, and I think tonight is their last night. Would you mind if Georges and I stole Bev and Wayne for the evening? We'll bring them back tomorrow."

Francois had just lifted Pearl's last concern. "If they would like, I don't mind. We won't have much time to share tonight anyway, and I'd rather they had a good time."

"Great, Mom," Beverly said, hugging her mother. "We'll see you in the morning."

"See you tomorrow, Mom," Wayne said, also giving her a kiss. "Enjoy!"

She watched the four walk off. Just before they reached the edge of the shelter, Beverly turned. There was no mistake in her silent words. *I love you.* Pearl knew she had made the right decision.

She and Bob danced two more dances as the crowd gradually thinned. The party was going to be nothing like last night, but she didn't care. She was dancing at last, in both body and spirit. Whatever steps Bob chose, she moved easily into it. Then the strains of the old waltz "After the Ball" filled the air.

"This can be a difficult one," Bob said. "Want to give it a try?"

She looked at Moland, who was standing too far away to hear the question. He smiled and nodded. "Why the hell not?" she said. Maybe the happy juice talking, maybe not.

She felt like a queen as he led her to the floor and into a simplified Viennese waltz, which she easily picked up. As the music played, they danced. She was unaware of those around her, and he seemed to feel at ease. As far as she was concerned, at that moment, it was only she, he, and the music. As they twirled around the dance floor, she glided free on the air currents of life. She sensed that they were meant to be a team. As this rendition slowed to its melancholy end, she summoned the courage to do something she had never done before. Her heart pumped with anxiety; sweat popped out all over, including the palms of her hands. "Would you like to go for a moonlight walk on the beach? It's a beautiful evening."

"I'd like that very much." He smiled.

Moland stood in the shadows watching, grinning, and nodding his head.

* * *

The Shelter was empty except for the nuns, who stood looking at the gift. Sister Joan continued to admire it while Sisters Marie and Ester hid behind her, peering over her shoulders. They gazed at a bronze voodoo mask with crossed bones mounted on a blood red background and framed with interlocking pieces of driftwood. On each side of the mask's face, serpents connected the ends of the bones. The seven-stranded spiral hairdo was bordered by scaly horns.

The mask had two sets of ears. One set resembled a pair of angel wings, the other oblong disk antennas. Serrated lashes surrounded surreal eyeballs, and its nose resembled that of a lion, less whiskers. Jagged canines filled the grinning mouth, and from the chin hung a chicken's neck and head surrounded by a beard of spiraled hair. Growing prominently from the mask's forehead was the Christian cross.

The engraved inscription read:

THE MASKS OF GOD ARE LEGION

"Horrible!" declared Sister Marie.

"Awful!" growled Sister Ester.

"Wonderful!" exclaimed Sister Joan.

Jim Henry

EPILOGUE

Three Years Later

Domino, Eduardo's fishing buddy, thanks to many successful shore-to-ship runs, has a new boat and motor, and a comfortable one-room house near the beach with screens on the windows.

Girard Louis, one of Pearl's students, is in his last year at school, is the campus computer whiz, and is teaching the younger ones computer skills. He plans to go to college and major in computer sciences and information technology.

Jean Claude LaPorte, another of Pearl's students, graduated from St. Jude's, moved to Port-au-Prince, got a job in a bank. He began dating a very likable young lady who got pregnant and ultimately gave birth, but Jean Claude died from complications from AIDS, and his wife soon followed. The child is in a foster home, not doing well.

Michelette's mother, emaciated by cancer and nursed by Michelette, died a horrible, prolonged death within eighteen months after the appreciation party. Until the week before her death, she continued testing her daughter's virginity, which Michelette never again openly resisted.

Francois and Georges have never officially married. She is now Haiti's foremost artist. Georges has the most successful fishery business in Haiti and continues to lead the effort for better management of the country's natural resources.

Having computers brought in students who could afford to pay tuition, which has allowed the staff to give additional scholarships, including one to a child of the family Pearl visited with Moland.

Sister Marie's kind, gentle heart, not long after the party, raced into overdrive and failed before she could receive medical attention.

Sister Ester remains on staff and continues to wonder why Pearl's sculpture wasn't melted down and made into something useful.

Father Mike's youth still belies his wisdom, and he is following his life's dream of being the parish priest as well as schoolmaster at St. Jude's.

Sister Joan is still eating Natti's cookies.

Moland is too.

What about Pearl? Well, she signed the divorce papers and sent them with Wayne to mail in the States. Because no one was pushing, the divorce took about a year to wind its way through Florida's legal system.

From the weekend of the party until their marriage, Pearl and Bob made many trips back and forth. Finally, in a touching civil ceremony in Florida, their marriage took place. In attendance were all of their children, Bob's grandchild, and Pearl's—soon to be their—adopted daughter, Michelette, now one of the youngest students at the Sorbonne in Paris, majoring in art and mythology.

The religious leaders at the wedding? Father Mike and Moland, who else? Sister Ester and Sister Joan tagged along in civilian dress so as not to be too conspicuous. Natti and a couple of students held down St. Jude's the weekend everyone was gone.

Did Pearl continue to be a staff member? Yes, but only until the end of the school year after the divorce was final. Because her marriage had not been annulled by the Church, and in spite of all Father Mike could do, she was dismissed as an official member of St. Jude's staff.

But Bob's wife had died. He applied for, and got, the official position the day it became open. Naturally, his life's companion came along as part of the package and is now a permanent substitute at the same salary level as before. They live in Primal Hall, and Father Mike took Pearl's old room in the Nest. For supplementary income, Bob continues to operate his consulting business via the Internet.

The sculpture hangs in Primal Hall.

As Horús Esprit "Moland" Gúyon says, "God's spirit has many masks and moves in strange and mysterious ways."

Jim Henry

***When two souls love each other, they don't look at
each other…They look in the same direction.***

Antoine de Saint-Exupery

About the Author

Jim Henry was born in rural Florida in the mid-thirties. After serving in the infantry in Korea, he graduated from the University of Florida College of Engineering. He first retired from professional engineering in 1985, but has twice been enticed to return to the workforce. He retired for the third, and last, time in October 2001, but is still active on special projects. **Jim**, using his laptop, takes notes to use in pursuit of his avocation—writing.

Jim remains active in his community. He has served with many community organizations, most notably the Sarasota Education Foundation. He is an active Rotarian, (http://sarasotarotary.org) is a Paul Harris Fellow several times over, has recently completed a Rotary project in Haiti, and will be the Governor for Rotary District 6960 in the Rotary Year 2003-2004.

A minimum of 25 percent of the profit from **Jim**'s books goes to Rotary projects local and International, the Education Foundation of Sarasota County, North United Methodist Church, and the University of Florida. A minimum of 25 percent of the profits from Sins of Pearl will be used for the Caribbean Initiative, with special emphasis on projects in Haiti and the Dominican Republic.